THE DREAM IS FREE
BUT THE HUSTLE IS SOLD SEPARATELY

Kurt,

All the best
&

Much Success!

JK

THE
DREAM
IS FREE

BUT THE HUSTLE IS SOLD SEPARATELY

GEORGE "GK" KOUFALIS

Published by *George "GK" Koufalis*
P.O. Box 3157, Bethlehem, PA 18017
www.chaseyourvisions.com

ISBN 9780692861622

Printed in the United States of America

Library of Congress Control Number: 2017904169

This book is for everyone who has ever had a dream.

TABLE OF CONTENTS

ACKNOWLEDGEMENTS

This book, like all significant undertakings, would not have been possible without the inspiration and support of so many others. I am deeply grateful for the special touch and care that a precious few have made, and are continuing to make, on me that helped shape the book you are now able to hold.

To my mom, Irene, who has been both a mother and father to my brother Christos and I growing up. She always did everything she could to raise us the very best she could despite being a kid herself. She taught me to not be afraid to be different and to stick to what I believe and never give up. As such, many of my best qualities come from my mother. I certainly wouldn't be as successful without her guidance throughout my life. Any time I second guessed myself, she pushed me to keep fighting. I am grateful for all she has sacrificed for me and my brother.

To my grandmother, Tina, who is the foundation of my mother's family. She came to America for a better life. I respect how courageous she was to leave everything behind in our native Greece for the possibility of a better life here in America.

To my gorgeous life partner, Monica, who always believes and only sees the best in me. She is as beautiful on the inside as she is on the outside. I appreciate, beyond words can express, how understanding she is of my crazy ways and how she never trys to change me.

To my friend, Brian, who flew from New Mexico to Pennsylvania to visit and inspired me to finish this book. You gave me the nudge I needed to finally make it a reality. You are one of the kindest and most unique people I have ever met. I thank you for that.

To all single mothers—it's your strength and love that allows life to thrive. If you gave up like so many fathers do, this world would be a much different and scarier place. Thank you for being the glue that holds it all together and the warmth that makes it worthwhile.

To everyone who I've been fortunate to have our paths cross as well as those who tried to keep me down. I am blessed with countless supportive people in my life, especially everyone in my network marketing business—I appreciate you all. We all meet people for a reason, a season or a lifetime. All of them are here to teach us something or help us move forward. In life, we must do everything twice, once in our minds and then again for real. Since you are reading this, it is real and you are part of my life.

And the biggest inspiration for this book...

To my beloved grandmother, Yaya, the most selfless and loving woman I have ever known. Her love was the most powerful and tender I've ever felt and the very inspiration for this book. I would give anything to spend 10 more seconds with her for just a hug and a kiss. I miss her so much! My love for her grows in the sacred space she will always hold in my heart. I can't thank her enough for showing me that love truly conquers all. I think about her cooking in the kitchen making such amazing recipes. If love can be eaten, it would be by her hands. I know she's proudly looking down on me. Until I see you again on day...

INTRODUCTION

I would like to share with you a story; it's the story of my life. All of us are equally important as human beings. My life is no more important than yours. The only difference is that I chose to write my life down and share it. I consider sharing our lives with others as a gift. The gift in this book will give you the knowledge and tools to grow with. It will demonstrate that you can overcome adversities and enhance your positivity in life. More importantly, it will help you act with clear purpose and intent. No matter where you may currently be emotionally, it will add value to your life and help you to achieve a positive mindset.

My hope is that this book will be one of your most valuable resources for resiliency and personal growth. It is written in two parts. Part one takes you on an intimate look at my story and life's many challenges from dark nights of the soul to the normal everyday variety. I certainly didn't always have the success and happiness I do today. In truth, most of my life has been anything but that. Part two will instruct and guide you through my 21-day program that we all can benefit from. If I had just written the book with the 21-day plan, it would likely be categorized as another self-help book. You may think: who is this guy and who is he to give me a plan? As you already know, life itself and the School of Hard Knocks is a lot tougher than what the "system" makes it out to be. The system is school, parents, authority figures, and what others tell us growing up. It is said that no one hits harder than life. The key is to know how to avoid the blows and know you'll overcome them.

My hope is that, by reading my story and how I was able to transcend my past, you will be inspired and armed with the tools to triumph over your challenges. My goal is to bring out the best in you and help you live a happier, more fulfilling life. In knowing my story, you too will know that your past or present does not have to equal your future. The exercises in the hands-on part of the book will give you an easy step by step method to follow so you stay on the proverbial Yellow Brick Road and make progress.

Writing this book was way outside my comfort zone. For starters, I have never written a book and grammar has been my Achilles' heel all my life. Thankfully, there are people that are good at that stuff. Even more challenging is that I am a very private person and most of the information in this book, I haven't even shared with close friends or family.

I have learned that when we feel scared or uncomfortable it is also a sign of something that can be great on the other side of the fear. All my fears in life have prepared me for this moment. It's through the fear and pain that we can teach and help others. It is these same crippling emotions that will give us more strength for the next stage in life. Courage, after all, is defined as perseverance despite fear, not in the absence of it. Jack Canfield said it best, "Everything you want is on the other side of fear."

This book delves into my past but I have learned to not live in the past for too long. My goal is to empower you to not allow negativity to take up space in your mind. Your mind can either think of the life you desire or the life that you are not happy with, it can't think of both at the same time. Remember you are where you are today because of all thoughts and choices you have made. My wish is for you to think of the life you want. I believe if your problems consume you, your goals in life are too small.

Knowing that I can positively impact at least one person is the reason that compelled me to write this book. This book is not about comparison between your life and mine. It's about the importance of facing your past, becoming more self-aware, and focusing on your future. We must understand that we are responsible for our lives no matter what has happened to us up to this point. To grow, we can no longer use our past issues as an excuse to stop us from creating a new way of thinking and living.

Ok, it's time to get started. Let's go.

CHAPTER 1

YAYA'S LOVE

My life on paper reads like a person who should have been a failure or just another negative statistic. Surprisingly, I run into many successful people who, on paper, had no chance. I knew at a young age that being a so-called statistic was something I would never accept. Everyone in life goes through tough times, some worse than others. I've learned that tough times don't last but tough people do.

Some of the worst beginnings makes for the best endings. We can't go back and change how it all started but we can change how it will end. Being alive a new day means you can have a new start. Do I wish I had a better past? I do! Sometimes I daydream of traveling back in time and changing my childhood, but that means the present might not be as good as it is. A different past would mean a different present. That present wouldn't be the one I have now. Therefore, I accept my past as the challenge to make me who I am today. Because of the past that I endured, I may not be the man who helps other people today. I leave the past in the past and I encourage you to do the same.

I believe past issues in our lives get us ready for a higher level of living.

And as the saying goes, "To whom much is given, much is expected." How can I lead anyone if I have never endured hardship? It would not be possible. I believe bad things happen to good people because only good people can turn around and make something positive out of it. All we have is the now and the now is the only moment guaranteed. If we spend too much time worrying about the past, we lose the enjoyment and growth of the present. The windshield is bigger than the rearview mirror for a reason. It's because we are not headed in the past, we are headed forward. If you drive looking in the rearview mirror you will lose out on the amazing things in front of you because you won't see them. You will also eventually crash. Easier said than done, I know! Speaking of the past, let's start looking at mine, so you can understand me better.

I was born in Allentown, Pennsylvania on April 12, 1975, to Greek parents. My parents got married when my mother was 14 and my dad was 19. My mother was 16 and my father was 20 when I was born. Due to being young, overwhelmed and not financially sound, I was sent to Greece at the age of three to live with my dad's mom, Diamantina. I can recall being dropped off at my great aunt's house and my mother not coming back that night. It felt like ages since I had seen my mom. I learned as I got older it was actually 13 days since she had dropped me off. To a kid at that age, 13 days is an eternity!

My parents were having personal issues and neither could take care of me, so while they tried to figure things out, off to Greece I went. I can still recall my dad and my brother's godfather taking me to the airport. The only memories of that trip I still remember is my dad telling me to hold this lady's hand

and that she will take care of me until I got to Greece. I realized as I got older it was a flight attendant. I sat with the flight attendant and she helped me find my grandmother when we arrived in Athens.

Times were very different back then. Could you imagine the backlash if someone did that today with their kid? But I also believe some of the kids of the past generations are the most resilient adults now due to the way we lived in those days. I remember holding her hand and feeling safe, though not sure why, perhaps because I missed my mother. The only other memory I can recall from that day is taking a taxi with my grandmother to her house. I recall this because I was vomiting in the backseat and she was hugging me telling the driver his stomach must be bothering him. To this day, I still get motion sickness and must take motion sickness medication when traveling.

As you may imagine, all this instilled a feeling of abandonment in my life and a high degree of independence. The abandonment has always made it tough for me to get emotionally close to people, especially love interests. There was always a fear of them just one day leaving because things got tough. The independence, on the other hand, has been a gift and a curse. The curse is that I feel more comfortable living alone and being introverted most the time. This makes it challenging developing greater commitment in relationships.

Yaya in Greek means grandmother. Until the day she passed away on July 22, 2014, I called her Yaya. My grandmother was the kindest woman with the biggest heart. I owe who I am today to her selflessness. I can still recall sleeping in bed with her in Greece and she seemed like a giant to me. She was only about 5'3" but at the age of three, she seemed like a tower. I pray as I get older, I never forget my early experiences with her.

We had an outhouse for a bathroom and I remember in the middle of the night for a few days, I had my grandmother awake all night and outside in the cold with me. I had gotten a urinary tract infection at the age of four and I had to use the outhouse at least a dozen times that one night and my grandmother realized something was wrong. My grandmother went outside with me every single time and was so kind about it. When she realized something was wrong, she took me to the hospital, where they explained what was wrong. That hospital was so scary. I never experienced a hospital before then. I know those early examples of love and caring have had a huge impact on why I have empathy and a huge heart.

At the age of four, my parents asked for me back, as they had worked out their issues for the time being, so I returned to America. Prior to returning to America, I recall my mother used to call me occasionally. There was a corner store that had the only phone on the block. When she would call, the woman from the store would send someone to yell in the street that my mother was on the phone. I knew somehow it was my mom and that she loved me but for some reason, I was supposed to be in Greece. It was hard to understand as a kid, maybe I understand now and just think I did back then?

The other moment that sticks out during this time is me running around the streets of Athens and in empty buildings with my older cousins all day being mischievous. I don't recall flying home but I do remember being at the airport in America. My mother picked me up with her little sister. I recollect they were both crying their eyes out. I wasn't sure why but today I understand they were tears of joy. I was just quiet, I knew it was my mother and it felt good to be back but at that age, I was still trying to make sense of it all.

Greek was my first language which made the start of my education difficult and made me a target for bullying. I was enrolled in English as a second language and worked with the school aids to get me on par with the other children in my academics. Some of the kids, who were a clique of bullies, would call me Greek Geek in elementary school for the first few years. Considering I used to run the streets of Athens at four years old with my older cousins and flew back to America by myself, I never just took it when the other kids taunted me.

I had already forged a strong leadership personality in Greece. To make the teasing even worse, my mom's mom, my other grandmother, Tina, owned a small diner and had fired one of my elementary classmates' mother. So that student came to school and told everyone my grandmother's diner had roaches and not to eat there. I went from having a peaceful life in Greece with lots of love to going to a place everyday that I didn't like. School was my least favorite place to be. And to further my distress, I had a disruptive family life as my parents started to have marital issues again.

This was my first look at a world of pain once returning to America, a world which I had never experienced before. I would come home and tell my mom what was going on at school and how I was being bullied and being called Greek Geek. One day, to my surprise, my mother gave me a pin that read Greek Power. It was huge and it had a white background with blue letters. She told me to wear it on my shirt and wear it proudly when I went go to school. So the next day and every day for a long time, I wore that pin. I felt like Superman and no matter what the kids said to me, I didn't let them bother me. The kids who bullied me eventually gave up because I wouldn't give up fighting back. This is the reason why today my Facebook page and my home-based business are both named George K Power. I never forgot how crucial my stance against opposition was during those unforgettable days at Jefferson elementary school in Allentown, Pennsylvania.

To this day, I think about that phrase on the pin and it gives me strength when I need it. We are always going to have people who attack us in life. The greater the cause in your life, the bigger the opposition you will experience. If you study history you see this repeated over and over again. As you create your mark in the universe you will have negativity thrown at you. You will have haters, but if you take a stance and persist, in time, you will have admiration instead.

The events in the following chapter taught me that people will dislike you for simply being different and you must never allow them to win. As I have gotten older, being Greek has actually been a great conversation starter. I have met several people who have Greece on their bucket list. I still face this resentment from people who feel the need to attack me just for being successful. Happy and successful people don't do this. It is the unhappy people who see something in you that they wish they had and out of the insecurity of their own inner sense of lacking something, they attack you. To this day, I have never met a hater doing better than me.

Someone, somewhere, sometime will surely talk badly about this book. I already have come to expect it. But without all the bad things that have happened that I've written about in this book, I wouldn't have been able to be the person to even write a book. I need these people for a greater purpose, which allows me to help more people. Remember, what feared you, prepared you. The person doing the attacking wishes they had the courage to pursue their dreams. Therefore, they must fixate on your success and try to bring it down to feel better about themselves and validate their situation.

In life, there are two ways to create success. One way is to follow the lead of someone you admire and build what I call a success tower like them. Or instead of putting in the work to build your own success tower, you find it easier to knock another person's tower down in the hopes to bring them to your level, because you don't believe you can build your own tower. The latter will only hold you down, not them. The other lesson I learned is if you stay positive and work to rid your life of negativity, it will eventually subside. One hundred percent of the things that bothered me in the past don't even matter today. They all worked themselves out. Some took much longer and were more painful but in the end, they don't matter. I keep this in mind as I encounter daily challenges. Next time something happens, I ask myself, "Will this matter a year from now?" Almost all the time, the answer is no, and I prevent myself from being worked up or unsettled. It's a great technique. I recommend you give it a try. It'll not only keep your blood pressure down, it'll also help prevent potential damage to a relationship or prevent you making a bad decision.

———————

CHAPTER 2

HEAVY HANDS

I didn't know it then but looking back now, I grew up in a disruptive and abusive environment. My parents divorced when I was nine years old. My mom asked me when I was eight if I would be okay with her divorcing my father. I had never heard of divorce and didn't know any other kids who didn't have a dad at home. I said, "Mom I don't want to not have a dad even though dad hurts me." My dad would discipline me by one method. That method was a Mixed Martial Arts (MMA) beat down. The difference is it's an MMA fight between a kid versus an adult, if you know what I mean.

I can still recall occasions where he body slammed me, broke my lip, and broke a toy plastic gun over my head in the name of discipline. He would always be in a bad mood and the slightest thing would set him off. In one instance when I was 6, I was sitting with my brother who at the time was one year old and I was calling him John instead of his name Chris. My dad overheard me and yelled at me saying, "Don't call him that, he will grow up thinking his name is John." Then he broke my Mr. T hard plastic gun over my head. The worst part was that one violent act always triggered him to attack me two or three times. In that instance, he went upstairs and came back down with shaving cream on his face to yell at me again for making him mad. He would punish me for getting mad in the first place. As you might imagine, I hated my life between the ages of five and nine.

I felt like I was always walking on egg shells and tried so hard to not set him off. If you looked closely, you would notice a slight black and blue bruise on my face on my first-grade pictures. I cannot recall the reason for that beating but this was the only one he ever apologized for. I remember him coming upstairs into my room and saying sorry as he sat next to me.

In those days, people didn't get involved in violent or abusive family matters like someone would today. In today's world, you pinch your kids and the cops are arresting you. It has gone to the other extreme. My dad was unhappy with his life and most of the time he just took it out on me. My brother was only two, so he didn't get any of it at that time. But as badly as he treated me, he was worse with my mom.

One time she ran out of the house and he was pulling her to try to take her back in the house to hit her more. There were two elderly women pleading with him to let her go but they were old and I could tell they were scared. As I watched from the kitchen, my friend who was over said let's go to my house. Instead of following her, I ran to my bedroom. She had begged me to go with her but I wanted to go to my room so I could pray. I had a figurine of the Virgin Mary above my bed that I used to pray to every night before I slept. I remember the ache and desperate longing while begging Holy Mary to please make my dad stop hurting my mother. I can't remember how that fight ended but I do recall that it was the beginning of the end of the chaotic family life. Very soon afterward was when it all came to a head and, ultimately, an end.

The fights got bigger and more frequent between my parents. There were even times my mom, grandmother, and siblings were all in the house fighting my dad like the Royal Rumble you see in World Wrestling Entertainment (WWE). Back when I was a kid, America didn't have all the domestic violence awareness we have now. There were several times the cops were called to my house. Every time, there would be two cops. One for my mom's side and one for my dad's side. They would write down some notes and just leave until they came out again the next time. As a kid, I always thought that the cop on my mom's side" was the nice cop and the one on my dad's was the bad cop. It's sort of comical now that I think about it. As kids, we do the best to interpret what we see.

It was time again for my mom to ask me that big question. A year later, at nine years old, she asked again: "How would you feel if I divorced your dad?" It was a lot of pressure being asked that question. I felt like it would be me who caused them to divorce. But the pain of him staying in the home was too much and I said, "Please divorce him." So soon after that, my dad was gone.

My father didn't make it easy, though. He once broke into the attic window and as he was coming down the steps, I heard the loud footsteps and screamed and my mother called the police. The neighbor identified him climbing up the house. Now it was just my mother, my three-year-old brother Christo, and I. So, after seeing my father hit my mother repeatedly and being a victim of his beatings, I felt peace for the first time since Greece.

As mentioned earlier, my dad had an unusual temper. He would hit me, go do something, and then get mad again because I got him angry in the first place and the onslaught would continue. This would usually go on in a series of three sets. I was always expecting to get beat three times per incident. It got to the point where it didn't even hurt physically anymore. I would even fake cry so he would stop. It hurt emotionally and I didn't understand it at all.

In my dad's youth, he left Greece on a ship for work at fifteen. He was one of six children and he left Greece to make money and help his family. One day in New York, he decided not to board the ship again and moved to Easton, Pennsylvania instead. That's where he met my mother, as she was waitressing along with her mother at a diner. My dad gave my mom a dollar tip, which in 1973 was big. He asked my grandmother if he could marry my mother and she said yes. My mom told me that she thought he was cute and that she was already raising her three little siblings, so she thought being married to my dad would be easier and she would be happier. She told me that on their first date, my dad decided to let my mom try to drive his stick shift car in a parking lot. She had never driven a manual vehicle before as she was only fourteen but he said he would teach her. Well, she didn't do too well, stalled the car and my dad slapped her in the face. No matter how many times I have heard this story it still puzzles me how she would have continued to date him. Although if she didn't, you would not be reading this now.

On the other hand, my mother moved to America at nine years of age. She did not have an easy life before meeting my dad and, I believe he provided her an escape. Even though it wasn't ideal, it was the lesser of two evils, so to speak. After my parents divorced, I saw my dad once a week on Sundays. There were many years, I didn't see him at all. When I would see him, he would order pizza and go take a nap while my brother and I waited for the day to be over so we could go home to mom. We kept each other busy and ran around with him doing the things he wanted. It always felt like he had us over because he had to out of obligation.

He never watched me play any of my sports. I played soccer, football, baseball, and karate. My mother put me into sports after my parents divorced, hoping it would help with structure. The last time my dad hit me was when I was 12. I was visiting him for Father's Day and he asked me why I only got him a card. He said: "Where is my present?" I said I didn't have one and he punched me in the stomach, knocking the wind out of me. After that, I stopped going over to see him. My mom wouldn't send us knowing we were unhappy. He was okay with that.

My biggest disappointments were that my dad never saw me graduate high school, college or win a bodybuilding contest. When he didn't come to my high school graduation, I didn't speak to him for a few years. As an adult, my relationship with my dad is not perfect but we talk and I see him every few months. My grandmother in Greece, his mother, always pleaded with me not to ignore my father. Her pleading is the only reason I would resume the relationship every time, after years of distance. It is for my grandmother and stepmother that I make the effort to work on our relationship. What would we ever do without mothers and a woman's touch!

The wiser, older me knows that keeping a grudge or being angry is like stabbing yourself in the heart every day thinking it will hurt the other person. The other person usually isn't even thinking about you and you're only hurting yourself. I have learned to forgive my dad and I accept him for who he is. If things had been different, I wouldn't be who I am today and I like who I am. Forgiving my dad didn't help him, it helped me! That's the power of forgiveness, it heals the forgiver.

My stepmother and my dad are today, surprisingly, a part of my home-based business. They are using it as a supplement for retirement and that has been bringing us all closer togeth-er. Forgiveness and personal growth are incredibly powerful. My dad and I are different people today than we were. Not only have I forgiven him but I am also grateful for his role in my life. I believe his and my experience can help others find peace. The man that he was is not the man he is today. I respect him for being my dad and giving me some of the tools that fashioned the man I am today.

Today, my dad is a wonderful grandfather to my neph-ew and that shows me he has also grown as a person. I can still recall promising myself as a kid I would never grow up to be a dad like him. I see now my dad had his own hardships and challenges which I can look back now and say were a big rea-son for his behavior. He also had some great attributes. He was a hard worker, provided for his family, fixed everything in the house and took pride in his skills as a chef. Today my father is in his sixties and is much calmer and still one of the hardest-work-ing guys I know.

Many of you might be able to relate to this. I respect my dad because without him I could not exist and I know he's proud of the man I have become. Although I never needed his approval, it is always nice to have it. Forgiveness is not for them, it's for you. It shows how secure you are with yourself and it gives you the ability to take the power back. It shows that your mind is so powerful that you can forgive. I point all this out because there are so many people that continue to carry unresolved issues and baggage. No one can resolve them but yourself. The best, most loving, liberating and rejuvenating thing we can do is to simply put the luggage down. You never know the weight of a burden you carry until you set it down.

I do believe the love of my grandmother, Yaya, in Greece was the foundation of the loving person I am despite going through that painful ordeal growing up. If I never had that experience of Yaya's love, I would be a very different person today. Everything happens for a reason. It's all part of the process of life.

The events in everyone's life help shape who they are and all the events I shared with you have molded me to be a strong person who fears no man but God. They have taught me to know what I want to be as a father when I have my own child. I believe I will be an amazing father and break the cycle, which statistically is hard to do. But once again I refuse to be a statistic. I do have a bizarre temper and have been known to go from zero to 60 in a second. As part of my commitment to personal growth and being a work-in-progress, I'm blessed that my temper has never resulted in anything serious. I have learned to use my knowledge more and my temper less. I know some of you have the same problem but admitting is the first step and talking about it is the second step.

This chapter stings a bit because I see that little boy in my mind and I couldn't help him back then. But it also is healing and fulfilling because I know many people are carrying their own crosses, endured trials and tribulations, and still battling to free themselves emotionally and mentally. This chapter was for you. That boy is alive and well today and that is what I wish for you.

CHAPTER 3

HERE WE GO AGAIN

At long last, there was peace. And it was well-received. But as the tide goes out, it also comes back in. So the peace that arrived at long last was short to stay. About two years after the divorce, my mother remarried. My stepfather was not physically abusive but he was controlling and verbally abusive. My mother and he are now divorced and have been since about 1998.

She tells us that she married him so there was a man in the house. To this day, I have a hard time accepting that because she stayed with him even though he didn't like my brother and me. He was very jealous of my mother's relationship with us. She was not allowed to do nice things for us or buy us gifts. If she did she would have to hide it from him. My brother and I were not allowed to play with each other either. He had a daughter who was a few years older than my brother and she was never nice to us. My brother and I were always so nice to them. We wanted him and his daughter to accept us. We wanted a dad so bad and hoped he would take that role but it never happened. I remember him always drinking beer, staying at home, and making up rules to punish us.

Our stepfather would try to audio record us and set up traps to see if we disobeyed him. He would call me a loser and tell me that I would grow up to be nothing. I find that funny now because looking back my mother supported us all financially. I remember one year I accidently found his tax return and he made $12,000 dollars that year while my mother was making six figures. I can say I have never had a positive male role model in my life growing up.

By my mid-teens, my mother and I grew more apart as my stepdad controlled everything my mother thought and did. I always felt like he somehow had brainwashed her to pick him over her own kids. I had the feeling by 14 that no one cared. I ran away from home a few times. Unfortunately, my mom's mom didn't want me to live with her and my friends' parents couldn't keep me. So I was forced to return.

I got myself involved with the wrong crowd because I became angry. I started to shoplift at stores, damage property, and get into fights. I remember thinking I wanted to get caught so I could go to a juvenile detention center to leave my house. I also now started to learn about sex from the wrong people and fell victim to the attention of older women. At 16, I got arrested but not quite the way I was hoping too.

I started lifting weights at 15 and by 16 was as built as a grown man. My brother and I have always been blessed with muscular genetics. I started to feel powerful and started sticking up for myself when my stepdad attacked me verbally. My stepdad was a huge man. He was 6'3" and probably weighed 270 pounds. But I could tell he was starting to think twice when he saw me. I started to carry a gun in my car that a friend had given me which made me feel safe.

One day, as my stepdad started on me, I said I have a present for you and asked him to open his hand. I dropped nine bullets in his hand. He didn't say anything at that moment. A few days later something started an argument between us and I lost my temper and had enough. I got a metal baseball bat and stood at the bottom of the stairs and yelled up to him. I told him to come downstairs because I was going to kill him. He didn't come out of his room.

The next day, my mother told me that she wanted to talk to the State Police to help us as a family. I agreed to go but didn't know it was a setup. After a few minutes of the officer asking me questions about guns and not liking my answers, I was arrested for terrorist threats against my stepfather. I was beyond angry and couldn't believe my mother went along with it. She told me she had no clue they would arrest me. My stepdad tricked her too.

Here I was now, 17, on probation for six months and having to take urine tests with other teenagers who were all arrested for serious crimes. Out of this came something great. As it turns out, life is not without a sense of irony. I had peace again for the first time in my life. My one aunt saw an episode of the Oprah Winfrey show and it talked about problem teens moving out on their own. My aunt suggested to my mother that she help me get an apartment for my last year of high school. She wasn't really for the idea but my stepdad saw it as a possible way to get me out of the house for good. My mom agreed and I got a 1-bedroom apartment a few blocks away from school. She paid the rent and I paid for my food, gas, and other needs. I couldn't let my probation officer know this, so we used my dad's address as my residence.

My last year of high school was so peaceful. I was alone and away from abusive men in my life, once and for all. My attendance at school was almost perfect and I was working at a car wash to support myself. I worked as a busboy at the age of 15 and bought my first car on my own. I have always liked working and making money. At one point, I worked two part-time jobs in high school: at a gas station and at a bowling alley.

The events in this chapter have helped me to be a good male role model to children. My current girlfriend has a son and I make it my duty to be a positive role model in his life. I was angry with my mom for almost two decades about me being arrested at 17. However, once I started to self-educate by reading several books on self-improvement, I learned to let it go. Something I thought I would never be able to do. This is the reason I know we can all let the past go with the right knowledge.

———————

CHAPTER 4

THE WOUNDS THAT HEAL & THE SCARS THAT DON'T

This part of the book is my least favorite to discuss. I try not to think about the moments of my life that I'm about to share very often. There were many years where it affected my emotional and romantic intimacy with women. It's a topic of sexual intimacy and it's a private subject, one I never discuss, but these are usually the discussions that can help others. So I have decided to take myself back to some days previously tucked away.

My first recollection of sex was around when I was 11 years old. My grandmother bought the diner my dad owned when my parents divorced. In the bathroom for 25 cents you could buy something called love drops and French ticklers, you know the kind. Like all kids, I loved any machine that you could insert money into and buy something. My curiosity got the best of me so I purchased both of these items and showed my friend who lived a few doors down from me and was a little older. He told me it had something to do with when men and women make babies.

At the time, my uncle was staying at my mom's home and he was diagnosed with a mental disorder. We asked him about men and women making babies and he told us the man sticks his penis in the woman's hole and that's how they make babies. I didn't believe it and told my friend that my mother was right, he is crazy.

A few months later, my friend and I stumbled onto an enclosed trailer at the local baseball field where we found all types of magazines. To our astonishment, there were about 50 Playboy magazines from the 1970s. We ran home and got a paper bag and took them all. I hid them in my room and started to examine them. I was aroused for the first time although I wasn't sure why. I was mesmerized by these women. If I recall correctly, they were nude but not X-rated. You could see their breasts and pubic hair without much else below. This was the beginning of my understanding that there were things to learn as I started to get older.

There was some kissing at school and a little touchy-feely stuff at a few girls' houses, not to mention a few kids bringing in some X-rated magazines to school, but up until this point, I look back and think it was normal boys discovering their sexuality. I started getting so involved in sports that after that first year of all this stuff, I barely gave it another thought.

That all changed when my mom's cousin from New Jersey moved to Pennsylvania and started to spend time with us. The first unusual experience with her was when I was 13 or 14 and she was about 30. I was lying on the floor sleeping and she started telling me to wake up. As I woke up, I looked up and she was standing on top of me wearing a long white open-bottom robe. I looked up and I could see she had no underwear and I was looking at her vagina. I didn't know what was going on but I was in shock. She asked me if I liked it and I didn't answer. This type of stuff went on or a few years. I remember her calling me into the bathroom and showing me her vagina through her pantyhose.

As an adult, it makes me angry because I know that was very wrong but at that age I was very confused. I didn't think it was right but every time she showed me her vagina I got aroused, which I had never felt before. One day at her mom's house, she asked me to come into a room in the basement where she had a pornographic movie on the TV while everyone else was upstairs. She told me to watch it with her and said that if she wasn't my mom's cousin, she would have sex with me.

I was now much more aware of my sexuality because of this. A year later, I was intimate with a girl from school and when the condom broke, I was petrified. I was so scared that I didn't have any more sexual experiences for a whole year. The next two sexual experiences ruined my chances of having a beautiful intimate experience in the future and with someone whom I could love before having sex. I still battle with the effects to this day.

A friend from school had a mom who was more like a friend to me than a mom. She used to smoke pot, party, and be very open about sex. One day when I was 16, I was sitting on the sofa and she sat on my lap and I got aroused. She made a comment like, "That feels good." Keep in mind that at 16 I looked like a fully-developed man. I had facial hair and was more muscular than most average adult men.

That experience made me start to have a crush on her. She was probably around 33 and I had already been familiar with older women from my experiences with my mom's cousin. At this point, I couldn't even relate to girls my age. I was mostly attracted to older women now.

One night, I ran away from home after a fight with my stepdad and I went to my friend's house. He went to bed shortly after I got there and his mom and I started to talk about my home life. She mentioned a barber she had been dating was coming over her house at midnight to have sex with her. Well at midnight, she realized he wasn't coming over and was very upset. She told me how he would always stand her up. I said to her, if you were my girlfriend, I wouldn't stand you up. The next thing I know, she grabs my hand and we walk through a room where her two daughters were sleeping and into her room. I can't remember how it started but we had sex.

I remember afterward she took me in the bathroom and told me to wipe myself off and to always do this after sex. After that night, she started to ask me to pick her up to help her run errands and she would always wear a short dress with no underwear. She would have me take her to a park to have sex in my car. One day her son and I were talking to a few of our friends and he said, "Guess who my mom is dating? George!" My jaw dropped and I must have turned bright red. I think he must have figured something was going on by how his mom was dressing and how many times I was running her around to run errands.

This lasted for only a few months before she passed me on to her 25-year-old friend. She told me she couldn't do it anymore but her friend wanted to be with me. So for the next few months, I was sexually active with her. I started to get feelings for her and one day I came over to my friend's house and found out she had slept with another guy the night after me. I was devastated! I realized she was using me and didn't care about me.

I ran into my friend's mom at a night club a few years ago,

and she whispered in my ear how she thought I grew up to be a very sexy man and she taught me everything I probably knew. It was the first time I had seen her in 18 years and it really freaked me out. I heard the other lady, who she passed me to, had died.

After this whole experience, I didn't feel the same anymore. It actually made me feel dirty and confused. When I was in school, I felt like I couldn't relate anymore and I was holding a dirty little secret. If this wasn't bad enough, it got even worse.

I hadn't seen my mom's cousin for a year or two. She moved back to New Jersey. I can't remember why I went to visit her. I think her three kids, who I used to spend lots of time with when they lived in Pennsylvania, wanted to see me. I figured since it had been a while since anything weird happened, and her kids would be in her house, I could go visit and be okay.

I drove to New Jersey and everything seemed normal. Everyone went to sleep and I was still awake. She asked me to talk to her and fill her in on my life. I remember her getting a bottle of wine out and pouring us both a glass. I had never drunk wine before and never drank at all. I can remember getting drunk and her asking me to go in a hot tub in the master bedroom with her. The next thing I knew, I was out of the hot tub and on her bed. She was on top of me having sex. I also recall going into the bathroom and wiping myself clean afterward and when she saw me, she said, "What the hell are you doing? You think I am dirty?" She was angry and I was nervous. I passed out right after that and woke up the next morning alone in the room. I stood up and walked out to the upstairs bathroom where I could hear her on the phone.

She said, "It was so disgusting, he's like my cousin." I felt the most upsetting feeling throughout my entire body. I started to get myself ready to leave and was going to sneak out of the house to go back home. She then comes up and says good morning like nothing ever happened. She tells me she's going to run out and be right back. After she left, I grabbed the phone and dialed *69 to see who she spoke to but I got scared and hung up. I got in my Suzuki Samurai and started on my way back home to Pennsylvania.

Forty minutes from home, my engine blew up and I was stranded on the side of the road. I was so angry and upset; I started to walk home on the highway. After about half an hour of walking, a couple pulled over and asked if I needed a ride home. I made it home safely to my apartment and called my mom to tell her what had happened. She told me that her cousin was a sex addict and she had slept with my mom's husband and her sisters' boyfriends.

I have not seen my mother's cousin in over 20 years. Last I heard, she was arrested and in jail for stealing an elderly woman's life savings that she was caring for. The elderly woman had a heart attack and died when she was informed that everything she had was gone.

Writing this chapter makes me feel sick to my stomach. The only positive thing I can say is if, and when, I have children, I'd make sure they are protected from all this dysfunction and abuse. Because of all this, sex never felt right for many years and I didn't enjoy it. I felt like I couldn't trust women and that I had to always be in charge and be dominating to be in control. Meaningless sex for many years is the only way I could enjoy it. I felt I had to be emotionally detached and wouldn't allow any partner to be on top of me during sex unless I chose to have her there. I always equated that position with my mom's cousin.

How am I today? Can I have intimacy and enjoy it with someone I love? It's much better through much personal growth and self-development. Even though I fight it, I still get flash-backs. Those feelings never completely go away but they have lost much of their grip on me with time.

When I am in love, those feelings are still there, but I focus on the love. For me, it all comes down to the discipline of knowing the right way to share intimacy with another person. They say time heals all wounds but if the wound itself is not taken care of it never heals. I keep striving to get farther and farther away from those feelings. I don't have to be 100% better. I can still be happy and accept it as part of a learning experience that I may not understand, but that one day I will.

Due to the love I experienced and was shown early in my life from my grandmother, I am kind, loving, affectionate and sweet. People may be able to strip us of some things but we are not fully broken. If you have ever been sexually used or abused, don't allow it to stop you from shining. We can't let them win. The new person who loves you in your life is not them. Give them a chance and allow yourself to be at peace.

CHAPTER 5

TIME TO BE AN ADULT

Eight weeks before graduating high school, I broke my leg in a freak car accident in my friend's driveway. I also broke my ankle my freshman year during football practice for the William Allen Canaries in Allentown, Pennsylvania. I decided to start focusing on bodybuilding and put football on the backburner. It's funny; I started and ended high school on crutches. The only cool thing about breaking my ankle is that the kid who tackled me went on to the National Football League (NFL) and won the Super Bowl with the St. Louis Rams. That's the closest I ever got to the NFL.

My friends on the football team tried to convince me to try out my senior year for football again. I was 195 pounds and about 5'10" and one of the strongest kids in the school. I tried out for the team and was running through people in tackle drills. The coach wanted me to for the starting linebacker position. After the first week, I had muscle soreness so bad in my calves that I could barely walk. I had also lost a few pounds and started to think it would affect my size I had worked so hard to gain. I decided to take a few days off from football practice. The coach told me that I would have to run laps for missing practice. No one in my family even knew that I was trying out for football. That summer, I already had my own apartment. The absence of anyone ever making me accountable led me to quit. Our football team went all the way that year and I watched from the bleachers. To this day, I know I should have run those extra laps and never quit.

Breaking my leg my senior year changed the direction of my life. I was already sworn in with the Navy to leave for Great Lakes Michigan after high school. I signed up for the buddy system with my friend when I was 17. He lived a few doors down from me during the years my dad lived with us. I spent lots of time at his house because his father treated me like his own kid. I used to pray for a dad like his. When we moved to my stepfather's house, I barely saw my friend's dad anymore. My leg couldn't heal fast enough and I never left for the navy. I had signed up for two years and was planning on moving to California to pursue underwater welding. I believe things in life happen the way they are supposed to. I wasn't meant to go away. I decided to start at business college with the friend who had left for the Navy. He had been discharged during boot camp and had come home. I did the school thing for a year and I got bored and didn't like it. I also felt stressed, as I was adding more debt in student loans to my name. What made my decision to quit was when I found out the pay for the jobs available after graduation.

I got a job at a gas station and bowling alley instead. I worked a lot and I loved working and making money. Back then I believed if I worked as many hours as possible and all holidays, I would be living like a king. I found out very quickly I was stuck in the rat race. I started to get very down and fell into a depression. I got let go at the gas station job. Someone was stealing cigarettes, so they made every single person working a shift count all the cigarettes and write down the total for their shift. I did it for a few days but I was not happy about it. I didn't smoke and disliked cigarettes. There was usually about 1000 cigarette packs to count. The one night I had counted around 700 packs and I got distracted and lost count. I decided I was no longer going to count cigarettes. I left my boss a letter about what had happened and how I was not going to start the count over again. I took the next few days off because I injured my back and during my time at home, I was notified not to come back anymore. Soon after that, I left the bowling alley and fell into a deep depression. My mother helped me with my bills for a while and then she told me that I should just move into my stepfather's house, since it was empty.

My stepfather still had his house from before he met my mother. As much as I didn't want to even think about my stepfather, I decided to take my mother up on her offer since I was broke and depressed. I moved into that house thinking it would help me work out the issues that I was dealing with. My entire life of pain all somehow hit me at once at the age of 19. I started going to counseling with my mother's offer to pay for it. I did it for six months and then one day my mom called me and told me something that changed our relationship. She told me that my stepfather wanted me out of the house and he didn't want my mother to help me anymore.

My exact words to her were, "If you do this, you're no longer my mother and I will never speak to you again." I now had to find a place to stay and quick. I reached out to my aunt's ex-boyfriend who I considered like an uncle. He had been in my life since the age of 10. They dated for about a decade and we had become good friends. He told me I was welcomed to stay with him. While staying with him, I let my driver's license expire and decided that I didn't want to be part of the outside world anymore. My depression now had turned into seclusion and isolation.

I left the house only two times in eight months. I had to leave once because I cut myself by accident and needed to see a doctor and the other time for a haircut. I used to sit in my room during the summer and see people walking to the local festival and I felt like a prisoner in my room. Mentally I didn't feel right anymore and didn't like it outside the house. Both times I left the house, I got car sick while in the car.

Then one day I started getting these weird compulsions to think about stuff over and over. My brain started to analyze everything and anything, I felt like I was going nuts. If someone would come in the house and pick up a picture frame or set their keys down, I would think: what makes them think they can do that? Anyone who would walk by and pat me on the back would make me think: how can they touch me without asking? I started to write all these things down and I could never come up with an actual answer. There were no answers to these questions.

I was very fortunate that my senior year high school girlfriend and I got back together after breaking up for a year. She decided to help me through this tough part of my life. She worked three jobs to support herself and me. She would bring me food every week and did all she could to try to help me get better. She bought me some books to read and a weight set to start working out. Looking back now, I can say I didn't deserve her in my life. I added no value to her life and was not always the nicest guy to her because of my mind being all over the place. I believe she held on to the fact that I was her high school love and that kept her in my life. This is a part of my life that makes me feel embarrassed when I think about it.

Today I am a strong warrior who can handle just about everything, relatively, but there was a time that I was weak and lost. I was at the kitchen door one day and I saw 11 guys come out of a van with guns. I told my aunt's ex-boyfriend that I think he may have some friends coming to the house with guns. I looked back and he was running to the bathroom. Next thing I knew, his two dogs in the yard were being maced and I was being thrown on the floor and handcuffed. They had a search warrant for the house and a warrant for his arrest. He went off to prison and sold his house and all his furniture and put the money in a trust. This way when he got out of prison, he could start over with his life.

I decided to move into my girlfriend's mother's house. Her dad had moved out and her parents were divorcing, so her mother let me move in the basement. I stayed there for a year and was then told it was time for me to find another place. The entire time I was not working and still having crazy thoughts. I felt stuck in life. My mother somehow found out where I was and reached out to me by dropping my little brother off to see me. I hadn't seen him in two years. I hadn't spoken to my mother in two years. I found out my mother was going through a divorce and my stepfather had gotten very mean and ugly towards her. I decided to go see my mother when she asked me to move back in with her. Soon after, I moved in with her and every morning we would talk about my thoughts and the pain of her divorce. Soon I started to feel well enough to get my license renewed and after two years, take a bagel delivery job. I was far from better, but I was on an upswing for the first time in a long time.

This period of my life showed me that it's the little things that get us. This is called the compound effect. We often wonder how our life falls apart and how we get ourselves into bad circumstances. It's the little, sometimes tiny, daily activities or habits we do that create our advancement or our crash. Our minds are our biggest window of opportunity or our biggest demise. It's the little things that catch up and get us. It's so hard to get out of a downward spiral because our mind gets weaker and weaker and we start to think differently. During this period in my life, I actually thought I may lose my mind and never be the same. I used to pray that I could feel normal again.

In the next chapter, you will see that I forced myself to deal with the pain and eventually I was back to my old self.

CHAPTER 6

BACK TO WHERE
IT ALL STARTED

My brother just finished 11th grade when I was 23 years old and we decided to go to Greece together and have a fun summer. I hadn't been to Greece with my brother since he was four and I was nine years old. I was still living at my mother's house and doing much better.

I was working and going to the gym and the exercise was really helping me feel good again. The only issue I still had was that I would get bouts of the obsessive thoughts from time to time. Sometimes it would last for only a few days and other times for a few weeks at a time. I had to fight it by not letting my mind get into the circular process of over-analysis. It was much less frequent than before and I had faith it would go away. So, my brother and I arrived in Greece and stayed at the new house my father had built for himself when he retires.

The house was empty and we couldn't believe we were in Greece with our own house and we rented mopeds to get around. My brother and I had booked tickets for 12 weeks. In total, we were together for almost 6 years, off and on. My girlfriend was still the girlfriend I had in my senior year of high school. I bought her an airline ticket to come visit me after 10 weeks so we could spend a couple weeks with each other and then fly home together. I was excited that she was finally going to get a chance to meet most of my family and see where I grew up.

One morning about two weeks after arriving in Greece, I rode my moped to the little shop that had these red England-style pay phones for the tourists to use. I called my girlfriend back home as I did every few days. When she answered the phone, she didn't sound like her usual happy self. I asked her if everything was alright and she said no. She went on to tell me that she was not coming to Greece and that she felt free without me. I remember thinking, this must be a joke! I was in shock and felt like I was going to pass out. I never saw this coming after six years.

From the first year we met, we spoke about one day being in Greece together. She was the first girl that I loved and I was very hurt. More importantly, we were friends for a few years before we ever dated. That friendship is what allowed me to feel comfortable being in a romantic relationship with her. I was depressed every day for a month and time in Greece seemed to slip into slow motion. I thought about what she said every day. I would have my friends back home telling me that she was out at night clubs in little skirts dancing on boxes. It felt like someone had a knife in my chest and kept digging it deeper. About six weeks later I called my mom and my now ex-girlfriend was there having dinner with her.

She got on the phone and started crying and asked me if I thought we should work things out. As much as I loved her and wanted to, I couldn't. I felt betrayed and had started to feel better by this point. My exact words to her were, "So you broke up with me over the phone while I'm 5000 miles away. You have been going out partying, being seen with guys around you. I am here in the most beautiful place and I have beautiful girls from several different countries who find me desirable. I think I will stay single. You should have thought of that before you dumped me." After that call, I told myself I knew she would realize that she would regret what she lost once the excitement of the new attention wore off.

I started to allow myself to enjoy Greece soon after this call. My brother left in the 12th week to start the 12th grade back in America. I decided to stay in Greece for another six months to get over the breakup. I also felt like I wouldn't have many chances in life to be able to live out of the United States for six months.

I worked as a bartender and my brother worked as a doorman. About a month after my brother flew home, I got laid off from my job. The tourism started to slow down and they made some cuts at the bar. The entire time I was in Greece I worked out at a gym near my house. It was on the third floor of a building and had no air conditioning. It was brutal! The healthy Mediterranean diet, the swimming in the ocean and all the training had me in the best shape of my life. Greece started to get colder and all my friends who worked on the island were flying back to their countries for the winter.

Corfu, Greece is tourist destination from May until October. From November to April it's a ghost town. What I haven't told you is that my crazy compulsion of over-analysis I mentioned earlier came back with a vengeance after my girlfriend broke up with me. I had a journal and I would run into the bathroom at work and write anything that I questioned during my shift at work. The bar was so busy that I couldn't analyze what I wanted to while working. So, it was like I made a deal with my own brain. If you let me write it down, I promise to analyze it later when I get home. I tried dating a few girls but it was difficult. I would be listening to them and at the same time trying save things they said to think about later. Even during intimate moments, I couldn't fully enjoy them.

Then one day, I met a girl from England who worked on the island. She was intrigued by my accent as I was the only one in that town who was from America. Everyone in Greece called me the American and would say I sounded like the people in the American movies they watched. Most of the people working in Greece were visiting from Great Britain, Sweden, Italy, and Germany. We started to spend almost every night together and talk about life. It was not an intimate relationship since I didn't want to romantically be with another girl that way while in Greece. I explained to her that after a few months of girls asking me to take pictures at the bar or to take my shirt off all the time, I felt angry.

It's interesting, when all that first started to happen, I loved the attention but after a few months, I would get mad when a girl would ask me to pull up my shirt or take a provocative picture. I started to feel like everyone was superficial and no one wanted to get to really know me. I also explained I had something wrong with me and I didn't know what it was. She asked me to explain what I meant. So, I told her thinking she would call me crazy and never see me again. Instead, she was curious and wanted me to tell her all my thoughts that bothered me.

For the next few weeks, every night we spent about an hour going over everything that my mind came up with and wrote down that day. Every night she would give me the same answer, "There is no answer to that. These things that you're thinking about can't be explained." It was time for me to fly home and she was leaving for a small island near Spain to work for that winter. I told her that it meant a lot to me building our friendship and would love to have her visit me in America sometime. After 6 months, I finally flew home to America.

The events in this part of my life were bittersweet. I got a chance to spend six months with my Yaya and my family in Greece. It was also the best time my brother and I ever shared together. We talk about that summer to this day. It was also my first heartbreak and a time when my mind was not right.

If you are reading this and you feel your mind is not right, I feel your pain. It's a horrible feeling to know that you want to be your normal self but something, somehow, just isn't right. Being around people in Greece and working was much better for my recovery than sitting in the house like I did at one point. I forced myself to deal with the pain and not hide from the world was the only way I could get better. It may not have seemed like it on a day to day basis but I was climbing up towards recovery.

———

CHAPTER 7

AMERICA OR BUST

The fantasy world was gone and I was back in the real world. In Greece, everyone spoke English with an accent, and I barely heard profanity. I landed in John F. Kennedy (JFK) International Airport and the baggage workers were cursing up a storm as they spoke with each other.

I was taken aback and noticed that Greece had changed me because I was offended by the words I heard. I had made so many wonderful friends while in Greece. For about six months after Greece, I would write back and forth to my friends and then life got busy. The one person I kept writing with was the English girl I spent lots of time with towards the end of my trip.

I did three things when I got back home: got a job, joined a gym, and went to see a doctor. I got three jobs because I wanted to make a lot of money to go back to Greece. I worked as a personal trainer, a pizza delivery guy, and as a private investigator while also attending school. They were three very different jobs with nothing in common. I wanted to make more money and asked the gym owner if that was possible. He told me if I got American Council on Exercise (ACE) certified he would pay me more. I got excited and bought the books and started to study to take my test in Washington D.C.

One week before the test, we had a gym meeting with all the employees. The other personal trainer liked to wear golf shirts and I liked wearing tight V-neck shirts at work. Our boss decided we needed one shirt for everyone and I was okay with that. The other trainer who wasn't the nicest to me said well I'm okay with that but I am not wearing tight V-neck shirts I can tell you that. I felt embarrassed and was not happy about his comment. I went to my boss's office and told him my feeling. He told me that the other guy was there longer than me so no matter what I say, he's taking his side. I was furious and I asked him how much more money would I make once I pass my test and am officially a certified personal trainer. I couldn't believe his answer when he told me a dollar raise. All that studying for a dollar raise, you got to be kidding me! That was my last day of work because I quit.

My pizza delivery job was in the same town about 30 minutes from my house, so I quit that job too. The other trainer ended up secretly opening his own gym a mile down the road and it ultimately caused the gym I worked at to go out of business. I would have been one of his most loyal employees if he would have treated me and paid me like I deserved. I used to drive 30 minutes every day for seven dollars an hour while my clients paid him $70 an hour. Karma will always prevail and this is why I don't waste time being mad at people who do me wrong. Life has a way of always taking care of those people.

That same week, to add fuel to the fire, my ex-girlfriend who didn't come to Greece, informed me she had a one night stand the weekend she broke up with me. She told me she was at a bar and met a good-looking firefighter and went back to his place. One thing led to another as she was very drunk. She went on to say she woke up in the middle of the night and ran back to her hotel crying. She needed to get it off her chest. I was shocked because that was not the type of girl I knew her to be. She was also only 21 years old and I couldn't judge her actions. Surprisingly, it didn't bother me any more than the day she broke up with me. I realized I was over that pain, I was just happy she didn't tell me while I was in Greece.

After that conversation, we never really had friendly communications as we used to after I returned. That week, I also decided I never wanted to work for anyone ever again. I liked my boss at the private investigating job but I didn't want to build his dream anymore. I decided to give it a few more weeks for some money until I figure out what my next move was. But then a few nights later, he had me and another student from South America on a cheating case. We were in a van with night vision goggles trying to catch a woman cheating on her husband. I asked the guy on the case with me if he knew anything about the guy we were waiting for to arrive at the married lady's house. He told me he was a state cop and I remember thinking this is nuts. I can't spend any more time doing this kind of work, it's too negative. I called my boss and thanked him for the opportunity he gave me but explained I had to do something else.

I didn't necessarily know what I wanted to do but I knew I wanted to control my life and income. A guy I knew at the gym who was successful approached me and told me he had a business that believed I could make lots of money at. He told me he owned a traveling male review company and he wanted me to be part of his team. I laughed and told him, I can't do that. That night I thought about it and decided to call him and find out more. In Greece as a bartender, we used to strip down to boxer shorts once a week on the bar to the Full Monty movie song by

Tom Jones. After giving me some exciting details at 23 years of age about the income potential, girls, and freedom, I agreed to give it a shot.

I worked for the company for about six weeks and was making $200-$300 a night but didn't like it. The excitement he spoke of was a dark side that would take a vulnerable person on a journey towards destruction. The other performers were very sexually aggressive with the ladies in the audience. They would use Viagra, penis pumps and magazines to get excited before going out on the floor. Many of these ladies were married and their husbands were at home clueless. It just seemed wrong to me. I was super nice to all the ladies who came to see us. I would even have conversations with them. I was the oddball out, everyone would say. I never did anything sexually aggressive with them. It just wasn't my style. The other guys would have their faces in the women's breasts or would kiss them. Some women would say no to them which made me happy. I started getting a following and at times when other performers were dancing, they would chant my stage name. After a few weeks, some of the guys who were working there longer started to get jealous of me and tried to put me down. They would tell me I needed to be aroused before I went on the floor and that being nice is not what these girls want.

The one night, I saw a crowd of women circling one of the performers and I went over to see what was going on. I saw a customer performing oral sex on one of the guys who just performed. That was my last night ever doing anything remotely like that. I also had two women recognize me in public, one walking in a busy area of the city and the other in a department store. The one even had a Polaroid of her hugging me. I didn't want to go down this path. I knew where it would lead. I was very embarrassed and promised myself that I wouldn't ever do that again.

I was living with my mother and she had a book and it talked about the top businesses to start. I read through the book and the only business I believed I could do was lawn care. This is why I believe books are life changing. Books can give us knowledge from some of the smartest and most successful people to ever walk this planet. These books also have the entire lifespan of knowledge from these individuals. That book was inspired and educated me on my next move. I got a $1500 loan from my mother to start my business. I went to Sears and bought a lawnmower, a weed whacker, and a leaf blower. I also had 2000 neon green flyers made to walk around and stick on people's front doors.

My little brother told me he wanted to be part of my business, so we named it Lawn Brothers. The girl from England decided to come visit me after countless letters and phone calls. After the first few days, we decided to take our friendship to a more romantic level and we started to date. She, my brother, and I walked around the nicest housing developments and handed out 2000 flyers over a few weeks. I got a few calls and at 23 years of age owned my first business just like that.

After a few weeks starting the business, my brother left me on a ladder pulling off ivy from a brick house because his friends paged him to go hangout. It became Lawn Brother after that. I should have known that was going to happen. Most 18-year-olds are not prepared to run a business. When we would drive around, I would see giant lawns and say imagine how much money we could make on that lawn. He would barely acknowledge me and I could tell his mind was somewhere else. I was motivated and loved having my own business. My

English friend had to leave the country every three months for a week and then she was allowed back in again. Before she left for England the third time, she babysat for my mom's friend for a week. That lady gave her $200 and a nice card thanking her for watching her kids. She left for England for one week and then flew back. I drove to the Philadelphia International Airport to pick her up and I couldn't find her. Her flight had landed and everyone was off the plane. I went to the desk to ask about her and they told me she was detained and being sent back to England. They wouldn't tell me why and would not allow me to see her. When she arrived in England she called me and told me they read her card in her suitcase from the lady she babysat for and accused her of working in America without a worker's visa. She also had me write down a number that they stamped inside her passport. I called an attorney that dealt with immigration law and went to see her. She told me that the stamp was a denial of entry to the United States for five years.

The attorney said she would help me get her back in. After a few days, she called me and told me the only way to get her back in is if you fly to England and marry her. After that you can file paperwork and because she's your wife you can bring her back. We had only been dating for nine months and I was not ready for marriage. At the same time, I felt it wasn't right that we would be forced to break up. I felt that it was only right to fly to England and do what I needed to. It was still my busy lawn season and I had decided to get ready for my first bodybuilding show. So, for the next few months, we talked on the phone every day when I got home from cutting lawns.

Before she got to America the first time, I went to see a doctor who owned a bio feedback brain center. I was hooked up to all kinds of machines to try to understand what was going on.

It turned out even when I was completely relaxed my brain was a fully alert which was not normal. He explained that sitting in the house for almost a year and not leaving created obsessive compulsive disorder as a defense mechanism. Instead of my brain figuring out what had me so down it did the obsessive thoughts and compulsions.

Humans are social creatures; we are not meant to be in isolation. People have been known to go crazy by being isolated too long. He told me the same thing everyone else told me about my thoughts that there was no actual correct answer. He also showed me a book where ancient philosophers had a similar thought process as me. After a few weekly sessions with this doctor, I could go back to my old self. I recall a few times my brain trying to have an obsessive thought but I could shut it down quickly. It's been 15 years since the last time that's happened.

I ended up flying to England and living with my girlfriend's parents. I joined a gym and played soccer for Rolls Royce. They made the engines for planes out there. I became a huge Manchester United fan and enjoyed French fries with gravy and vinegar. The English people were very nice to me and liked the fact that I was from America. Almost everyone I spoke to wanted to visit America. We spent the winter in Barnoldswick, Lancashire, and some time in Blackpool and got married at the justice of the peace just so she could come back to America. My mother, brother, and good friend, Josh, all flew out to England for the ceremony. Josh really surprised me and we remain good friends today, especially since he's my barber. I appreciated him showing up and surprising me since many friends would not have done that. I am also proud of him for becoming the successful real estate entrepreneur and business owner he is today.

Josh came a long way from the high school days of cutting hair in his mom's bathtub. Having my family and a friend there made it easier to go through with. It's not what I envisioned marriage to be like when I was a little boy. I always saw myself falling madly in love and getting down on one knee and proposing to the woman I wanted to spend the rest of my life with. She and I both knew it was too soon but it was the only chance we had to continue the relationship and hopefully blossom into a true marriage. I returned home shortly after our justice of the peace ceremony and a few months later she joined me with no issues.

While I was waiting for her to come back, I injured my shoulder. I couldn't do any shoulder exercises. Six weeks later, one of my friends recommended a steroid that would heal my shoulder. I was against the use of steroids. When I lived in Greece, you could walk into any pharmacy and get them by telling the pharmacist it was for your grandma. Many of the guys in Greece used them told me that I had great genetics and if I took them, I would be a huge. I did my first bodybuilding show naturally and was planning on staying natural. I was hired shortly after my first bodybuilding show by Men's health for their 12-week Men's Hard Body Plan book.

I started acting classes and instead of an acting job, I got a modeling job. When I got called for the audition I had been pigging out for 10 days straight after my bodybuilding contest. I was eating Taco Bell when they called. I went in and they hired me but told me I had 10 days to get leaner. I ate zero carbohydrates for 10 days and came back ready for the job. I got paid $1000 a day for 3 days. I remember thinking about my $7 dollar an hour job and smiling.

The pressure now was on to continue my modeling and bodybuilding dreams. I enjoyed having my own business but it was not as rewarding to me. So, after six weeks of my shoulder not healing, I went to see my friend and he gave me an injection in my butt of a steroid. He told me to come back once a week for an injection. I didn't like needles and the thought of shooting myself with one made me feel anxiety. A few weeks later, my shoulder was healed and I was bigger and stronger than ever, I was hooked. I started to become aggressive and hormones were going crazy. It was overwhelming, to say the least.

My new wife was living in America with me and the pressure of being married without being ready was starting to get o me. I suddenly felt trapped and the steroids were not helping the situation. It enhanced all the arguments and made me someone else. I didn't even know who I was anymore but I just kept adding more and more different types of steroids to my weekly mix. It got to the point I was doing so many of them, I taught myself to inject myself. The marriage lasted for about two years and we split up. She decided to stay in America, eventually getting married and having 3 kids. We are still friends but we don't really talk much other than seeing each other's life on social media. I continued the next six years pursuing my bodybuilding and modeling dreams.

This chapter is all about taking risks. It taught me that with no risk there is no reward. Scared money doesn't make money. I gave up a good job for a great business, you must let go of something to obtain something better. We have one life to chase our dreams and that this life is not a "dress rehearsal." I rather fail forward and know I tried than to, one day, have regretted not trying. It also taught me that people enter our lives for a reason, season or a lifetime.

My wife and I helped each other in different ways. She helped me to start healing in Greece by listening to me. She also taught me that if ever get married again I need to be ready. I have never asked a girl to marry me so if I ever get married again, I'll know better. For her, I think, I was supposed to get her here to America to have a life here for some reason. She also has three beautiful children and has thanked me in the past. She said without us meeting, she wouldn't have had those children. Everything happens for a reason and it's there to get you where you need to be. Even if you can't see it at the time, which is true for just about all of us.

———————

CHAPTER 8

EVERY ACTION
HAS A REACTION

I was 24 years old and entering my first NPC bodybuilding contest. The NPC is the Mecca for amateur bodybuilding in the world. I took fourth place in a group of experienced body-builders and first place amongst the first competitors like myself. After the contest, I thought about why I didn't win the more experienced contest. I believed genetically I had the most gifts on stage but looking at the other three competitors ahead of me, it was obvious they were taking much more steroids and growth hormones.

I became obsessed with winning that contest and started to motivate myself by envisioning myself holding up the first place trophy. I started to study information on what I needed to do to manifest this goal. I made a plan and took action towards it every single day I woke up. These four steps are the steps that always lead me to success in any venture: knowing what motivates me, learning what information is needed, having a plan, and taking action. But even when you do everything right, you don't get what you want on your time. The universe gives it to you when it feels you are ready. I finally won that contest but it wasn't until three years later, after coming up short of first place three years in a row.

The contest was held at my high school 10 years to the date from when I graduated from there, which gave me even more motivation to win. I reminisced about my high school days, putting in work after school in the school gym. I remember in the 9th grade bench pressing 95 pounds and after a few repetitions it got stuck on my chest. My friends had to help me lift it off as they laughed. I remember going to the school gym with a cast on my leg and my friends helping me by bringing me the dumbbells. All these struggles and never quitting finally paid off.

Who would have known back in those days, I would be a champion one day and all the seemingly insignificant moments would lead to one of the best days of my life. If people truly understood that the days that seem the worst are the ones that create the best outcomes, they would never give up.

The following year I entered for the Pennsylvania state title and took second place. I now had a new obsession to be crowned Mr. Pennsylvania. So, I trained harder than ever and the following year I entered three contests. I competed in New York for the first time and beat out some of the best bodybuilders in the country. Once you win your weight class, the judges line you up against all the other weight class winners. I lost the overall to a competitor who is presently one of the best professional bodybuilders in the world. I also won the state title that year but lost the overall to one of the head judges' friends. I truly believed it was a political loss.

I loved bodybuilding but I was starting to realize it was subjective, political and unhealthy. I would lose 40 pounds for a contest and then gain 40 pounds when I wasn't competing. To get my body to appear as if it had no water under the skin the week of the contest, I would either take diuretics or not drink water for 48 hours prior to the contest. There were times that I was not on target for the contest; I wouldn't consume carbohydrates for a few weeks in a row to get my weight down. I would get blood work every 6 months to make sure I wasn't causing any damage to my body from the steroids and stress. My blood pressure was always high, my good cholesterol was always dangerously low, my bad cholesterol was through the roof and most of the levels were off the charts. My doctor would tell me that if I didn't stop, I would have serious health risks down the road.

I started to look 10 years older than I really was too. Instead of taking my doctor's advice, I told myself that I was immortal and I would be fine. I remember telling myself that I would not take too many steroids. There was no way that I would use growth hormones, thyroid medications, insulin or anything other than a few steroids. Well, I lied to myself because I started taking all of those performance-enhancing drugs to reach my goal of winning a state title.

I started to do lots of research and pick the brains of the bodybuilders who were on the level I wanted to reach. I found out that all of them were using much more performance-enhancing drugs than I was. The cost for those drugs was about $2000 a month, on top of all the special foods, traveling, gym memberships, tanning, contest fees and all the other expenses. I was only making $35K dollars a year; there was no way I could afford to be on that program. I found out that most of the guys who were on the next level of bodybuilding were selling these drugs to pay for their own habit. I was willing to do what it took to win and I started making some connections to buy these drugs cheaper. Many of them were being imported from Mexico, China, and Great Britain.

Overnight, I became that guy in the gym that could get you whatever you wanted. We are a product of who we spend our time with. I started spending more time with bodybuilders and less time with the people I used to know. The people you spend time with will rub off on you. Even if you think that's not possible, trust me, it happens. It sneaks up on you and the next thing you know, you're someone you don't even know. This is the reason I am so protective now of my space and who I allow myself to be around. Regardless of how self-improved I am, at any given time, I can regress by spending time with the wrong people.

In time, word got around that I had a great product and I was a reliable source. Soon I had a big clientele of local body-builders, summer warriors and the average Joe who wanted performance enhancement drugs or, as many know them, steroids. I started doing research and found out that it was much cheaper to get these drugs in myself from Mexico. I decided to go on a spring break trip with one of my friends with the intention of loading up on thousands of dollars' worth of steroids.

As I was walking down the street in Cancun, a Mexican man asked me if I needed drugs. I told him I was looking for steroids and he told me in the city the pharmacies had them the cheapest. I convinced my friend to take a taxi trip with me into the city. The city was very different than Cancun. It had police officers on mopeds with big guns strapped to them. The areas looked dangerous. My friend was telling me that he wasn't ever coming into this part of Mexico with me again. I had the taxi driver take me to three pharmacies and I went in and bought all their performance enhancement drugs. I bought some cotton swab boxes and packaged everything up when I got back to the hotel.

I had seen a FedEx while the taxi cab driver was taking us around the city. So, the day before we were scheduled to fly home, I hired a taxi cab driver to take me to a FedEx location. This taxi cab driver didn't understand English whatsoever. After 30 minutes of driving around, he couldn't find it for me. I ended up using a small Mexican post office to send them back to America. I had a connection who gave me money to send him steroids who said I could use his address. I spelled his name wrong and sent them to his house and used the hotel as the return address. When I got home he called me and asked me to come to his house. He showed me a letter that the entire supply was stuck in customs at JFK airport. We had two options the letter stated. Pay a $2000 petition fee and prove in court why we should have this returned to us. Or ignore the letter and they would keep the package but if another package comes to this address, they would press charges. We decided to ignore the letter and spend more money buying our performance enhancement drugs from the current sources we had.

Performance enhancement and steroids are interchangeable in the bodybuilding community. Performance enhancements cover a larger group of all the drugs used in sports. Some of the stuff we used was intended for animals—it had pictures of cattle on the bottle. We didn't care, we were all obsessed with the feeling these drugs gave us. I was bigger, stronger and faster. I was also moody, irritable, easily aggravated and didn't engage people in friendly conversation. It made me look great but also made me a complete jerk. It also gave me anxiety attacks and bouts of depression without any reason or cause. My obsession was so big that I started taking insulin and a drug called IGF1-R3. The growth hormones made me insulin resistant; therefore, I had to take insulin injections to offset that. The insulin also allowed me to consume and utilize much more food.

The IGF was an experimental drug that, in theory, allows muscle cells to split and double. This would allow for more muscle cells and with the use of steroids, I would be bigger than ever.

I was weighing about 270 pounds at about 5'10". My blood work was insanely off the charts. My testosterone levels came back at 12,000. The normal range for an adult male is 300-700. The lab tested it three times because they thought it had to be a mistake. In the end, they circled the number and wrote: must be a bodybuilder. My doctor told me that I was no longer human. My doctor had asked me if I was on steroids one day on a routine visit before I started getting blood work. I asked him what made him ask me that question. He told me because I had to walk through his door sideways. I admitted to him that day I was and asked him to help me monitor my health. I also would always tell him this is off the record. He agreed to make sure I didn't kill myself.

I had a few surgeries and was hospitalized due to all the drugs I used. The first one was called gynecomastia surgery. I had a hormone imbalance in my breast tissue that caused golf ball size lumps. I had to hold my chest when I ran because of the pain and they started to leak fluid. What made matters worse was that I couldn't compete because it looked horrible and it was looked down upon by the judges. Everyone was aware we took drugs to look like monsters but they didn't want us to advertise it. Having "gyno" was a walking billboard advertisement that you use steroids. High amounts of testosterone leads to an estrogen build up and that's how this develops. There are estrogen blockers but I think I took them too late and my testosterone levels were absurd.

My insurance wasn't willing to pay for the surgery because I wasn't overweight, they said. Many overweight men develop gynecomastia. I had a good friend who was a plastic surgeon and he was willing to do the surgery for me while I was awake. He had never done it anyone awake but I needed the surgery so I could compete in three months. I had it done for only $2000 and it was not a pleasant experience. The pain of that experience didn't match my quest for my goal. When I want something, I will go through whatever I need to for that goal. I was also hospitalized for sleep apnea. I had gotten so big that I would stop breathing in my sleep. It was either sleep with a breathing mask every night that sounded like Darth Vader or lose weight.

I was about to start losing weight because I could tell my body was not happy. I spoke to some other top level bodybuilders and they told me I didn't have to bulk up so much in the offseason. But before I could start cutting my weight down, I woke up one morning with a small dime size lump and hair missing around my hairline. I thought perhaps I strained myself and just ignored it. Within the next few weeks, my scalp was very red and my forehead had large veins protruding and I was forgetting things.

I was taking classes at a local college that year. It was my third attempt at college. Two years earlier, I applied and took the prerequisite classes and failed them all. I wasn't willing to take classes that wouldn't count towards me graduating with a degree. This time, I was willing to do it as I thought a degree would be a good backup plan to bodybuilding. I was having trouble in algebra so I hired a tutor that would come over my house. She would go over everything with me the night before a test and the day of the test I would forget it all. In addition, the headaches would be excruciating and that made concentrating even harder.

I was in school for about six weeks when all this started to happen. I showed up for an algebra test and the teacher wrote the test out in cursive writing. His handwriting was very difficult to read and I couldn't remember anything I studied. I got up and handed my test back to him and told him I was quitting college. He was concerned and told me, I could come back another day and take the test. I mentioned to him that there was no need, I can't come back. I went down to the main office to see the advisor to withdraw from school. She tried talking me out of it when I had a breakdown in her office. I explained to her something is wrong with me and I have to see a doctor. My college transcript today has 27 straight A's in a row, as I ended up going back to college for the fourth time, five years after this incident. But before all the A's, there were three W's for the 3 classes I withdrew from.

I went to see a good friend and workout partner and told him what was going on. He noticed the veins in my forehead and looked concerned. I told him my scalp was starting look different. His father was a doctor, so he had some medical knowledge. Up until this point, I was thinking it would all go away on its own. I was in denial and didn't want to believe, as big and strong as I was, that something was wrong with me. I told him what was going on and took off my hat. His face looked like he was seeing a ghost. He called his dad immediately and said dad something is wrong with GK. They believed it was some bizarre skin disorder and they got me into the top dermatologist the following day. This doctor had a six-month waiting list but the sense of urgency and my friend's dad got me in thankfully.

The lady that examined me before the doctor entered the room asked me if I had dyed my hair. I told her no I hadn't and asked her why she asked that question. She said that my scalp was purple. The doctor came in and put his hands on my veins near my hairline. He said, "I think you have an arteriovenous malformation (AVM)." Interestingly, I studied them somewhat in college. Your veins are pulsating like arteries do and that's not good. He told me I needed a Magnetic Resonance Image (MRI) as soon as possible. The next morning, I had an MRI and he was right. I also had something called a fistula along with the AVM.

I was then scheduled for an angiogram to see, more in-depth, what was going on. During the angiogram, I remember everyone in the room panicking as my blood pressure went so high it almost killed me. They were injecting medications into my intravenous bag to bring it down. When the report was returned, it revealed that it was a very rare form of AVM and the local doctor didn't feel comfortable trying to fix it. I was told this AVM could kill me and I could even die during surgery.

I started getting calls from major hospitals who were interested in seeing me to not only help me, but to make me a case study. I didn't want any part of being a Frankenstein. I went to Beth Israel hospital in New York to speak with a doctor who had written a book about my condition. After speaking to him and the other doctor from Japan, I felt I was at the right place. They informed me that the worst-case scenario would be that I could die or, once they repair the issue, that I could lose blood flow to my scalp and it would turn black and die off. This would leave me with a disfigurement.

I was scheduled for surgery in three weeks and I made sure I lost as much weight as I could and started doing cardio every day. I didn't want any blood pressure issues this time around. I remember signing a death waiver before I went into surgery, waiving their culpability if I died. The surgery was supposed to take two hours. They would enter through my groin and go up through my neck to my scalp.

When they got into my neck they couldn't get any further because my veins were very twisted and the device couldn't get through. They found another route and the surgery ended up taking four hours. The surgery was a success but I was left with a lump on my forehead from the glue type material they used to close off the improper connections. I also developed a blood clot in my calf. I was on blood thinners for a year and had blood work every 10 days.

I took a break from bodybuilding for a year but continued to model. In my pictures, you could see the lump on my forehead and it made me very depressed. I would ask my photographer to photoshop it out sometimes. Six years after the surgery, I got permission to remove that glue in my forehead from my original surgeon. There would be no health risks as it had done its job and was just in my body now taking up space. I had the same plastic surgeon that helped me with my gynecomastia perform the procedure. He made a small incision at my hairline and pulled it out with a surgical instrument.

To this day, we don't know if it was a genetic issue or something that formed from the experimental drugs I took for bodybuilding. I can tell you the few weeks leading up to the surgery were some of my darkest moments. I was thinking about all the worst-case possibilities and thought my bodybuilding career was over. I even thought I would rather die on my terms, not on an operating table. I even held a gun to my head and tried to convince myself to pull the trigger. My good friend had shot himself in the mouth three years ago, a week after we had been out having a wonderful time. I kept thinking about him and all the pain it caused people and I couldn't do it.

I think this chapter is important in the fact I had nothing good going for me at this point. At the time, it seemed like my reality but it wasn't. It was only my temporary reality. We tend to forget that when we get in tough places in life. I based my entire life on that year and that is the wrong thing to do. If I knew then what I know now, I would have been much more optimistic and less affected. I believe if my friend didn't kill himself, he would have had better times down the road. If I can go from pointing a gun to my head to today loving life more than ever and being successful, anyone can do it! It all starts with changing our thought process and understanding ourselves better.

CHAPTER 9

WE HAVE
A SEARCH WARRANT

It was a year after the surgery and the fact that I never won the Pennsylvania State bodybuilding title was haunting me. Seven years of hard work in the gym and all the sacrifices just to come up short didn't make sense. My doctor from New York told me that competing would most likely not cause another AVM, but he didn't recommend it. I thought about it long and hard. I decided I was going to give it one more try.

That year, I decided it would be a practice year and that the following year I would compete for the state title. Although it was a practice year, I still gave it my best and was hoping to win. I entered three contests and didn't win any of them. It was the worst year of my bodybuilding career. I felt like I had lost something after that surgery. Did I really give it 100 percent? Was my body not responding like it used to? I feel I lost some confidence after going through surgery and taking a year off. My mind was not as strong and when the mind fails everything else fails. The third show was a national level show in Cleveland, Ohio. I was projected to place in the top six at the weigh-in Thursday morning.

On Friday night, I looked at myself in the mirror and didn't think I was big enough to win. I ordered room service and ate a cheeseburger, french fries, and a cheesecake. I figured, if I didn't drink water, I would simply just look bigger and as tight. My mind started to play tricks on me. The next morning, I woke up and looked like a bloated mess. I placed 12th in the country instead. I was always my own worst critic in bodybuilding. Anytime I traveled to another state and didn't have my mirrors and my environment, I would sabotage myself. After the contest, I noticed a lump in my groin—turns out I had a double hernia. I had surgery and was out of the gym for six weeks. I ate junk food every day for those six weeks. I looked and felt horrible and was in the worst shape of my entire bodybuilding career.

It was now the first of January of the following year. The state title was in six months and I made the choice to finally let someone else coach me. I was not going to kill my efforts ever again. Plus, what I was doing wasn't working anymore. I hired a coach who had worked with some of the professional bodybuilders. His job was to determine what to eat, how to use my performance enhancement drugs and what to do in the gym. My only job was to listen and make the decision to win! The motivation was there, the information I had, the plan was set and I had the intention to take action. Coming off a six-week layoff from the gym and my diet due to a double hernia surgery made it a rough start. One of the hernias was from birth and the other from years of heavy weight training. I now was starting to believe that it wasn't healthy for me to keep using steroids. I was seeing other competitors in their 40s have kidney failure, heart attacks, and even dying.

I convinced myself this would be my last run. The poster for the contest even had big bold letters that read "NON-TEST-ED CONTEST". Everyone entering this contest was going to be maxed out on performance enhancement drugs. It was going to come down to who had the best genetics and more importantly who was willing to sacrifice and work the hardest. My coach would see me every two weeks and tell me what I needed to adjust. This was easier than trying to second guess myself which most bodybuilders do. It's hard to look at yourself in the mirror and be unbiased and truthful.

Four weeks before the state title my coach decided I should do a warm-up contest. The NPC Lehigh Valley Regionals was taking place in my hometown. The first two finishers would qualify for the Nationals and a chance to turn Professional. We figured I had a good chance of at least getting second place as I was about 85 percent of where I needed to be. The night before my contest, my girlfriend, who lived in Delaware, and I got into an argument and she told me she was not coming to my contest. She had been to all three contests with me the year before.

While I was on steroids, anything that happened always seemed more magnified. The little stuff seemed big and I would overreact to anything that would happen. When people say that steroids don't change them at all, they are in denial. There is no way that someone can take that many drugs that alter their body without altering their mind. I recall being angry that entire day because of her not showing up. Despite all the challenges and not being 100 percent ready for that contest, I won the entire contest.

There was a younger guy from Tennessee who should have beat me but he didn't know how to pose properly and was hiding all his best attributes. If you don't use your talent in life, it doesn't matter how great you can be, your ultimate best will not be realized. It was my first win since my AVM surgery and I really wasn't happy. I think I was starting to outgrow this sport. I think it was now more about a point to prove to myself than enjoying the sport.

Four weeks later, I won the Pennsylvania State Championship and entered a second contest taking place that day. The second contest allowed all non-Pennsylvania residents to compete from other states. I also won that contest and was the first person to win all those contests from Pennsylvania in the same year. I was undefeated that year and having a coach was a big reason for that. I had the potential and the gifts to be the best; I just needed someone to bring it out in me other than myself.

I finally won and asked myself: now what? The buzz in the industry was that I would be one of the professional bodybuilders the following year if I kept it up. I wasn't happy anymore, I wasn't even excited anymore. Not to mention during the contest another competitor elbowing me off the stage and we almost went at it backstage. I was tired of the politics and the ugliness of the sport. I was tired of the drugs and I was looking 10 years older than I was. My whole life revolved around bodybuilding and it was a selfish sport. I would miss family events because I couldn't be around certain foods. I would struggle to have a successful relationship because of the mood swings and self-absorption.

The steroids would also make me attracted to too many girls. My testosterone levels being so outrageous made it very difficult to be in a committed faithful relationship. I decided I had enough, it was over. I realized that if I didn't change my input, I can't change my output. I text messaged everyone who I sold steroids to and told them that I was retiring from the sport and they would need to find a new source for their drugs. That same morning, I decided that although college was not for me, I should do something new and positive. I needed new people in my life and a new goal. I walked into local college a few hours later to enroll. The lady informed me that I had to make an appointment and that there were no more appointments, and that school was about to start.

I remember getting upset and saying this was a stupid idea. Then I heard a woman call my name. It was a client of my mother's spa. She asked me what I was doing here. I explained to her what I wanted to do and she decided to not go on her lunch break and instead enroll me into classes. This woman will never understand how that small gesture of kindness was a big part of where I am at today. That was on a Tuesday and that Friday, the 8th of August, 2008, on the first day of the Beijing Olympics, my life was changed forever.

On the morning of August seventh, a good friend of mine texted me and wrote, "I know you're done with bodybuilding and selling but if you have anything left you don't want, I will take it." I had about $2000 of steroids that I wouldn't need. I told him he could come over that night and I would sell it to him but this was the end of it. He thanked me and that night he came to my house and bought almost everything I had. The next morning, on the eighth, I opened my mother's salon for her. I started working for my mother as well as in my business after I realized that cutting lawns for 40 years was going to be a rough life. I cut back on my lawn business to help run her business. The money in lawn care was good but I felt like I had bought myself a job that owned my life. It was an unpredictable business because it depended on the weather and it was very hard on my body and it was stealing the time in my life.

My mother was not aware of me selling steroids; she really didn't even know what went on in the sport. I was very fortunate she allowed me to work for her, so I could downsize my lawn business. I came home from my mom's business around noon—Fridays were half days. Then I would take a nap and around 3:00 pm cut lawns until 8:00 pm. I heard a knocking that sounded like the door was going to break off the hinges. I said to myself, whoever is knocking like that is going to get an earful. I then looked up at the surveillance camera and saw 13 government agents in two lines leading to my front door. I heard a loud voice saying, "We have a search warrant, open up."

So many things ran through my mind as I started walking down the stairs to answer the door. Everything seemed like a movie that was in slow motion. I remember having steroids and syringes on the dining room table. I thought: can I somehow get rid of it all? Should I run out the back door? Should I resist? I knew I was in trouble and my choices over the years had finally compounded and manifested into something very big. And then a sense of peace came over me and I told myself this is God's way of ending it all. It's supposed to end and there will be no going back now. I calmly opened the door and the agent with the gun looked unsure. I was huge at the time and in my underwear and my head was shaved. My presence was intimidating and he had no idea what I was going to do. After one second of staring, he tackled me and handcuffed me.

My house was swarmed with agents and neighborhood kids were outside yelling, "They're making a SWAT show!" They sat me in front of my sofa and I could see my school class schedule. I remember thinking I was so close to getting on with my life without getting in trouble. I even said to the agent, "Man, I was just going to start college. He told me he already knew that and knew I was on my way out. If you think about it, after eight years of drug use and a few years of selling steroids, it could have been a lot worse. I sat and watched my house get torn apart. I was leaving for Greece the following week to visit my grandmother before college started. I had $12,000 in an envelope and $3,000 of that was money my dad wanted me to give to my grandmother. $2,000 was money I earned from working and the other $7,000 was from steroid sales. They took it all, even the $100 in my wallet that was in my truck. My licensed guns were all taken along with some personal items, a computer, and pictures. I was then told to be ready to come to Harrisburg on Monday with a lawyer, and they left.

I called my mother, distraught. She ran over to my house and when she arrived and saw what happened, she was in shock. She took me to go to my bank and take out all the money I had as she was afraid it may also be taken. I also called my girlfriend from Delaware and told her I needed her help. We were off and on since the contest she never attended, but for winning it and her not being there, she surprised me by buying us tickets to Greece. I told her it was an emergency and she had to come to my house. She showed up that night and helped me clean up my house. I hired a lawyer and we went to Harrisburg on Monday. I was told I had to testify in front of the grand jury so they could prosecute me. I was not able to go to Greece as the court date fell on what would have been the third day of my trip.

I cried when I was told that. I had traveled to see my grandmother the last two years. She was 93 years old and I knew I wouldn't have much more time with her. That was more punishment to me than anything else they would do to me. The next year I went from hearing to hearing, from extension to extension. It turns out they arrested a couple in Harrisburg who were injecting their clients with steroids. That led them to the guy who came to my house the night before it got raided. He sold to an undercover agent which led them to me. The money he gave me the night before was from the agent and they found it in my room. I was set up by my friend. I have never heard from him or even seen him ever again.

Along the way, there was information brought to me that proved my illegal activities as well as that of a few other guys. I admitted to the information that was presented to me which proved my involvement with two other guys. In the end, about 10 people were arrested and convicted. The investigation had a second part a year later, which led to more arrests.

The man who was running for governor had it out to arrest anyone using or selling steroids. This was his ticket to be elected. They spent lots of tax dollars to bust all of us. I believe what I did was wrong and illegal, but there are much bigger problems they could have gone after than a few people injecting themselves with steroids. They decided to arrest me the day before Thanksgiving. They used my driver's license in which I was smiling on the front page of the local newspaper and on the local news. My phone started going crazy and so did my social media page. My grandma Tina called my mother and asked why I was smiling for my arrest picture. A good friend stuck in traffic called me to tell me I was featured on the highway billboard. It was a very difficult time for me on many levels. My name was now tarnished and I was coming off steroids cold turkey after eight years. I didn't have a chance to take myself off safely using the ancillary drugs needed. I had all that stuff ready but it was taken at the raid. People whispered, and I could tell they were talking about me while out with my friends.

While awaiting trial, I kept going to school and stayed low-key. I can understand why men who use steroids have a hard time quitting. It makes you feel so much more powerful. For those first six months after I got in trouble, I didn't know who I was anymore. My identity was a big, strong, larger-than-life guy who now was not considered a freak. My nickname was the Greek Freak and I liked it. I liked all the attention from people because of my muscular stature. Having kids point at me when I walked by them made me smile.

If I was in the gym and saw someone on steroids, I would get depressed and walk out and go home to sleep. It took about six months steroid-free for me to mentally feel normal. I could tell I was my old happier and nicer self that I used to be before bodybuilding. My hair got thicker, my skin was blemish free and I looked younger. I didn't tan my face for those eight years and didn't do recreational drugs or drink. Many of the people I knew who did steroids and competed tanned all year round and did other types of recreational drugs. I believe this allowed me to bounce back totally after six months.

The time came to find out my fate. I had a few things going for me. I was told that I was the only person who they arrested that wasn't caught in a lie. Many of the questions we were all asked, the attorney general's office already knew the answers. I had been a straight-A student with honors while awaiting my sentencing. I had letters from a few of my professors on my behalf. I was charged with five different crimes. A first offense for steroids is mandatory probation. I allowed the state to own my guns, so they could use them in their news segment where the man running for mayor explained how he got all these guns off the street. I had the guns because when I became a certified investigator at 23, I also got my Act-235 license. Along with that, I had certificates from the National Rifle Association (NRA) gun safety classes.

Those guns were never on the street but they used them to make their campaign look good. I was the most popular person arrested. I was the state champ, I was in magazines and I had a marketable look. I didn't fight the case, I took a plea bargain, had three charges dropped, and ended up with two ungraded misdemeanors. I was given two years' probation and 100 community service hours. In addition, my driver's license was suspended for six months as my conviction fell under the war on drugs rule. The gym I trained at told me I wasn't allowed to work out there anymore. The girlfriend that I had when my house was raided was no longer in my life. I had decided that due to the stress of us not getting along, it was best to be alone through the ordeal.

I want to clear something up to anyone reading this book who has read information that is not accurate about my case. It's been about a decade since this all happened and I still deal with issues from it. I was blacklisted among those who actively use steroids in my local community. To this day, many of them do not like me because I was arrested and quit that the scene. Many of those individuals, who were not even around at the time this all happened, call me a snitch. It's like that game whisper down the alley I was taught in elementary school. People tell other people a story and it keeps growing into what other people want it to sound like. The more successful I become the more they seem to get uglier towards me. Everyone can sit back and talk but until they are in that situation, they have no clue what they would really do.

This entire investigation started in Harrisburg, Pennsylvania, and through the guy who set me up. I was presented with facts such as phone conversations and videos and asked if that was me and two other guys in them. I answered yes, only a fool would say no to something like that. We all knew what we were doing had risks. Do I think if I answered no, those two guys would have my back? Of course not! Those two guys snitched on their own best friends, something I wouldn't have done. We were friends only because we dealt in illegal activities together. The story goes that I snitched on all the other defendants and all my customers. I never had any dealings with anyone else that was arrested aside from the two guys I mentioned. A dealer can't set up customers, he can only set up other dealers. Law enforcement doesn't give more drugs to someone they arrest to set someone else up. At least not at the level I was at.

I had never been arrested as an adult before. The first offense for a steroid arrest is probation. I took the plea bargain so that I would have fewer charges on my record and only misdemeanors instead of felonies. Ninety-four percent of all state cases end in a plea bargain. The court system wants convictions, money, and not to be tied up. Some people just don't think for themselves and want to believe other people's limiting beliefs and assumptions. Limiting beliefs and assumptions are what hold so many people down in life. If I hadn't turned on all these people, I wouldn't have had my face on the news and the front page of the local paper. I would have been kept out of the limelight as people who operate are.

One of the two guys that I did have dealings with is one of my biggest supporters these days. He promotes bodybuilding shows and although we don't hang out socially, I support him by advertising my girlfriend's hair salon on his promotional flyers. For the last three years, he calls me every three to six months and asks me to make a bodybuilding comeback and I politely decline. I have to give him credit for his persistence; persistence is one of the keys to success. He also only served probation as did every single person in the case except for one individual. He served about a year in jail for manufacturing steroids; I never had any illegal activities with that guy. He has gone on to have a lot of success as many of the guys I knew from the case have. I think for many of us, as bad as it seemed back then, it helped us alter our lives for the better.

The second guy in the case is still bitter about the entire thing. In late 2016, we saw each other for the first time in eight years. He saw me pull into a Lowe's and five minutes later when I came out of the store, my car was vandalized. He was gone and when I had the store look at the cameras, he was seen on camera near my car but the camera angle didn't have my car in it. Instead of assuming and getting revenge, I took the high road. After a few days, I found him and we spoke. He told me he might have touched my car but he couldn't remember. I took that as an admittance of guilt without admitting it. He was very bitter and I believe instead of using the experience for the better, he allowed it to take his life to a place he doesn't like. He is mad at me for admitting to the evidence presented to me.

The guy who went to jail for 11 months was his best friend. How did that happen? I'm sure you can take a guess. Until we stop blaming other people and our past, we can't move on. Honestly, I don't care what a small group of bodybuilders think about me. People in the real world that have more important things in life going on couldn't care less who got arrested for steroids and who told on who.

When I look back on how this muscular obsession started I can recall it. I was influenced watching the original Incredible Hulk series with Lou Ferrigno. I was amazed by how big he was when he turned green. My dream of being a competitive bodybuilder started at 14 years old. I was a fan of Arnold Schwarzenegger and many of the bodybuilders in the 90s. I was fueled by wanting to get so big and strong that no one would hit me ever again or mistreat me. I never expected it would devolve into a road of darkness. Once again, those seemingly small daily steps lead to something much bigger. Things can compound for the better but they can also compound for the worse. If you're reading this, you're either compounding upwards or downwards. No one stays the same in life.

The first time I used or sold steroids was no different than the last. The effort was no more or no less, it just compounded over time. It's the little things that get you. I didn't spend time with people using or selling steroids prior to me starting bodybuilding. I was influenced by these new friends without even realizing it. I am now aware of all my daily activities and how they will affect me. I am also careful who I allow in my space and what type of energy they bring. I didn't possess these powerful mental tools back then; I want you to gain those tools by reading this book.

I don't regret my choices in life because they have made me who I am today. If I had to do it all over again, I would have never used steroids. For me, the reward doesn't outweigh the risk. I urge anyone reading this to not get started if you're considering it, it's not worth it. If you're willing to accept the consequences that come along with it, then do what is best for you. If you're over 40 years old and need testosterone from your doctor for low levels of testosterone that's a different story. Everyone should do what's best for them. I just wouldn't have started it given the option for a redo. Life is not a dress rehearsal—you only get one chance. I now think about the consequences of my actions much more.

CHAPTER 10

YOU ARE NOT
THE FATHER

The case was finally over. Now it was time to overcome the challenges getting into trouble caused. I believed that I was being tested, I wasn't sure why, but I knew the universe wanted me to go through this. I didn't know how I was going to get through it yet believed that if I won at each day, eventually, I would find my path and get back to the top. So I embraced hitting rock bottom and decided to fight. I decided to move back home with my mom and this way, I was around a positive influence. I was also financially struggling with lawyer fees, court costs, fines and school loans. I had two more semesters of college to graduate and I had to hire a woman with a part time taxi business to take me to and from to school. I was broke with no driver's license and I felt like I was alone.

To make matters worse, I had to call a phone number to a drug testing place every night and listen for a color. If my color or all colors was called, I would need to go for a urine test to make sure I didn't drink or do recreational drugs. The man at the facility would stand there and observe me giving my specimen. It was embarrassing and I would sometimes be there an hour before I could give a sample. After a few weeks, I found a trick. The trick was to drink a few bottles of water right before they had me go into the bathroom. The facility even sold water in case people needed it. They were making money on water on top of everything else. After about three months of having clean urine tests, my probation officer found it unnecessary to continue. She told me my arrest was a joke to her and that steroids were not a serious crime. Surprisingly, I got that reaction from many people who knew what happened. It did make me feel better but I knew that a law is a law and I broke it.

I had a few things working in my favor towards a fresh start. My mother's spa was about a mile away from the house. Therefore, I could walk to work and home. It was wintertime and I didn't have to worry about driving for my lawn business. One of my friends from the gym and a co-worker helped me with rides to the drug testing facility, community service, and the grocery store. I had another friend who also owned a lawn service business and he wanted to start working out that winter, and he volunteered to take me to the gym everyday if I helped teach him how to work out properly.

I spent about 60 hours of my community service painting a gymnastics facility for kids. The other 40 hours were attending Friday night drug rehabilitation at a local church. I started to date again but wasn't ready for anything serious. I felt that I had a lot to learn about myself again. I started to date a girl who worked at the local pizza shop. She sent me a friend request on my social media page after I left the pizza shop. After about three months into it, I decided it wasn't going to work out and we stopped seeing each other. Then one day a few weeks afterwards, I was at the gym and I got a text from her informing me she was 16 weeks pregnant with my child but she was getting an abortion. I must admit I didn't believe her and figured it was a way to get me back in her life.

I was diagnosed with a Varicocele at the age of 23. It's a condition that makes it difficult and sometimes impossible for a man to have children and my condition was one of the more severe cases of it. The timing didn't add up either to me, so I told her to leave me alone and not contact me anymore. Two weeks later, I randomly ran into her, but I don't believe anything in life is truly random. We exchanged hellos and moved on. She texted me soon after I saw her and to told me that I looked good. I told her she looked good too and asked her if that workout program I created for her was working. She answered by telling me she was getting an abortion in a few days and couldn't workout. At that point, I asked her to come to my house that evening. When she came to my house, she had a pregnancy test with her but I put my hand on her stomach and I knew she was pregnant. She promised me that it was my kid and she had been with no other man.

I had just been to the Bodies in Motion exhibit and a saw a 16-week old fetus in a jar. That left a huge impact on me and I begged her to not get the abortion. I explained that I didn't have any kids and didn't think I could ever have one. This would be a miracle baby and she couldn't abort it. She still said no and that she didn't want it. I asked her how much more time did she have left before they wouldn't perform an abortion. She explained she could only go one more week. I asked her to give me that week and if at the end of that week she hasn't changed her mind then she could get an abortion.

I spent every day that week making sure I called her or stopped to see her at some point during the day. She told me she had seen a side of me that she never saw even when we were dating. She decided to not go through with the abortion. My mother was supportive and helped me get ready for this child. My mother and I were still in a bad financial state as business had been slow since the recession hit. We used our credit cards and built a baby room above the garage and connected it to my room. My mother also gave her a job at the family spa. We found out she was a high-risk pregnancy and I wanted her to be seated most of the day working behind the desk to avoid anything happening.

She had an ultrasound at the abortion clinic but they never told her anything about it. I went to her first ultrasound at the hospital and we found out she was carrying twins. I remember being excited and she was not happy at first and started crying. My family started pressuring me about a DNA test. I asked about getting one while she was pregnant but was told that it was too dangerous. She told me she would give me one the day that they are born. It was my first day of summer classes in college and that same day the water broke and I was rushing her to the hospital. It was time to become a dad.

The babies were born at 31 weeks and each weighed about four pounds. The mom told me during labor that I couldn't have my DNA test because it would ruin her special day. I didn't want to upset her and I decided to let it go for now. I signed the birth certificates having faith that I was doing the right thing. They had to stay in the Neonatal Intensive Care Unit (NICU) for nine weeks. I visited them every single day while they were in the hospital. The nurses told me that I was one of the only dads they saw there so much. They even made me a Father's Day card. I had to buy special car seats to get the babies home because they were so little. When we got home, the mother was very depressed and I took over many of the baby duties. At night, I would get up when they cried and spent all my free time with them. The boy was hooked up to a machine as he was not fully capable of being without it.

She and I started to argue and it became a very tough situation for me. It was obvious she and I couldn't be happy together but I didn't want to be a part time dad. In the back of my mind, I wasn't 100 percent sure they were even my kids. The kids didn't look at all like me and the fact that she wouldn't give me a DNA test made me suspicious. My family was pressuring me for the test and I was starting to feel stressed. On the Fourth of July, we had a party at my house and the kids' mom and I got into a huge argument. My family came into the room and my mom got involved in the argument. My mother demanded a DNA test or she would have to move. My mother got a DNA test from the local pharmacy and swabbed her, myself, and one of the twins. A few days later, I got a letter in the mail and it stated that I was not the father.

I drove to see the kids' mother as she was visiting her old job. I asked her to come outside and I told her what the results were. She started screaming at me that I was the dad and my mother got a cheap test from a pharmacy. I asked her to take a DNA test at the hospital and she refused. Later she came back to my mother's house where we were all staying. I told her I wanted her to leave but I would like one of the kids until she gives me a DNA test at a hospital. She wouldn't agree to this, so I agreed to let her have both kids until we figured this out. Her best friend started to think that maybe these really were not my kids. She felt bad for me and told the kids' mom that I had said even if the kids were not mine I would take care of them. I never said this but she said it in the hopes I would get the DNA test I wanted from her. It worked; she agreed to go give me the test.

She was now living at a friend's house with the babies. I had a feeling the kids were not mine but part of me was hoping it was a mistake and they were mine. I came home from work and there was a FedEx package in the door. I knew it was the test. This time I had both babies tested, not just the boy. I opened the letter and read the results and started to hyperventilate: I was not the father. I had had a week to prepare myself for this and calmly drove over to where she was staying. I filled my truck with all the baby things that I could fit in it. I also booked a ticket to Greece with my brother because I needed to get away. The pain was a new pain I hadn't experienced. I loved these two little babies as if they were my own.

I rang the doorbell and the kids' mom answered it and I asked her if we could talk. I told her about the result and that I deserved an explanation. She went on to say that she truly thought I was the dad. She recalls a night of drinking and going home with a guy she knew at the establishment. This happened around the same time we were just getting to know each other. She didn't recall it going further than a kiss, she told me she blacked out. I explained to her if she would have told me that from day 1, I would have still helped her. Also, that it would have been easier mentally during the process knowing the facts. I could have protected my heart until I knew for sure. If I had to speculate, I think part of her knew that I may not be the dad. She took a gamble and lost. Actually, I was the one who lost; it was one of the most traumatic experiences of my life. I didn't want anyone asking me about my upcoming fatherhood, so I left for Greece a few days after the paternity results.

I came back a few weeks later and for the first six months, someone would ask me how my twins were doing just about every day. I would wake up dreading running into people. Many friends followed my social media pages and they saw my posts as the pregnancy progressed and I built the twins room. I talked about being a dad with everyone I met and was so excited. This made it nearly impossible to get over it and it took a few years. The dad ended up being the guy she thought it was and after he got over the shock of the phone call that he was a dad, he stepped into their lives. The dad has never reached out to me but I met his mother once by chance. She broke down and cried as she thanked me for not allowing the abortion. She informed me she had no grandkids and her son wasn't planning on having kids. It was an emotional moment that made me feel good knowing I did the right thing. When the dad was proven the biological father, I still was responsible for child support as I had signed the birth certificates. I hired a lawyer and after a complicated and long process, I was released from the responsibility of child support.

I have spent about an hour with the twins one time since this whole ordeal took place seven years ago. Technically it was twice, if you count the time I saw them with their dad at a Starbucks, but they didn't see me. They wouldn't recognize me even if they did. It was surreal watching them with their dad, it felt like a dream. My mind didn't allow me to get upset; I didn't even have to think about what happened. I knew at that moment it all was supposed to happen the way it did. I allowed the mother to send me school pictures from time to time, which I enjoy seeing.

There is a lesson to everything that happens in life. I believe I was supposed to save two lives and feel that pain. I also think it will help me somehow in the future, I just don't know how yet. I'm learning that we are given pain at times in life to help others have a better life. I had a newly-developed corrective surgery on my Varicocele in 2014 but was given no guarantee it would work. Ninety days later, in early 2015, my current girlfriend and I got pregnant. Unfortunately, we miscarried at week 10. We were planning to announce it on my birthday two weeks later. It was a tough one for both of us but it made us stronger. One of my goals is to be one of the best dads on the planet and I am optimistic that will happen. My current girlfriend actually volunteered that if we ever have kids, she would want a DNA test to ease my mind. I think when I really become a dad, I will just know it.

CHAPTER 11

NETWORK MARKETING TRANSFORMED MY LIFE

I finally graduated with my Associate Degree in Business in May of 2011. It actually took 18 years from my first attempt at college until I graduated. I was very proud and excited to have finally graduated—and with a 3.9 GPA. I am also the first person in my immediate family to earn a college degree. I went out and started to see what was being offered in the job world. I was surprised to find out the starting yearly salary; it was insulting. During this time, I had friends with master's degrees who couldn't find a job.

Having someone tell me what I was worth was not easy, especially when I felt I was worth more. I did not spend thousands of dollars and the last four years of my life in classrooms to live paycheck to paycheck. I decided I would continue to work for my mother, cut lawns on the weekends, and take a few more classes to get my bachelor's degree. The idea was to stay proactive, and the added education wouldn't hurt. I was riding a wave of momentum with college and if I took break now, I may never go back.

My mom was about five weeks behind on my pay which was also making my financial situation harder. She wasn't charging me rent and helped me out anytime I needed it, so I just worked with her on my pay. I rewarded myself by taking my 1997 pick-up truck to a local paint shop and having it repainted. After doing this, I only had eight hundred dollars in my bank account. I was 36 years old living with my mother, driving a '97 pick-up truck, with $800 to my name, five weeks behind on getting paid and still on probation for another year. As depressing as it should have been, I was handling it well.

I felt that it was a better situation than the prior few years and it was only going to get better. I was making positive steps on a consistent basis and they had to pay off. I believed that if I made the right choices now, my life at 40 years old would be much better. The life we all have today is from the choices we made the past few years, not the choices we made in the present.

I have heard that there are two moments in your life that mean the most. The moment you are born and the moment you find what your purpose in life is. June 15, 2011, became the day I found my purpose in life. On June 14, my mother told me she wanted to talk to me about a business opportunity she had looked at the night before. My mom explained that her friend was involved in it and was trying to get her to look at it for over six months. She finally went to see it and believed that if I got involved I would be very successful at it. She also said it was one of the best opportunities she had ever seen. I trusted my mom's business sense and before the recession hit she was making money hand over fist in her business. Not to mention her spa, before the recession, was featured on the Oprah Winfrey show.

Knowing all this about my mother, I still told her I was not interested. I felt it sounded too good to be true and didn't understand why I had to pay $300 dollars to start. I also knew nothing about the company, the product, or the network marketing industry. I can jump ahead here and tell you that the $300 investment made me 7-figures back in less than six years. I also now realize that being skeptical and broke is a bad combination. I told my mother that they would have to pay me to do this stupid sounding business and I was done talking about it.

My mother, being Greek, doesn't give up easy; she went up to her office and came back down a few minutes later with a serious look on her face. She threw her credit card at me and said you're going to look at this and you're going to do it and it will be your early Christmas present. I told her I didn't want my Christmas present now but shook my head and agreed to call her friend and listen to her spiel.

Her friend started telling me about this business and although I didn't understand it all, I remember thinking it was a no-brainer. It's a great service, it saves people money, it won't affect what I am currently doing and the company is willing to pay me as much as I deserve. I liked the idea of helping other people and being part of a team. I know that a team, in any aspect of life, can always produce more than being alone. I always knew TEAM stands for Together Everyone Achieves More.

My friend who ran one of the local gyms had a lot of connections and I immediately called him and told him that I found something that would be huge. When I told him about it, he informed he had already started with this company the week before. He was planning on reaching out to me soon about it. I explained that my mother's friend wanted me to join her team. He asked me to join his team instead because the guys helping him were twin brothers and they were two of the best guys in the business. I remember thinking about a favor he had done for me in 2009 when my face was all over the news. When my gym canceled my membership and I felt like I had nowhere to go, I called him, not sure if he would allow me in his gym. Without hesitation, he told me I was welcome in his gym. I have never forgotten that favor; all my so-called friends had turned their backs on me. When I couldn't get them the drugs they needed anymore or only cared about lifting weights, they all disappeared. I told him to have one of the brothers come to my house the next day and if I liked them, "I will join with all of you."

June 15, 2011, started like any other day. I woke up and got ready for morning summer college classes. After the classes I came home and waited for one of the twin brothers to come by and show me this business in detail. The doorbell rang, I opened the door and recognized the guy from my local gym. He was sharply dressed and was driving a new luxury car. I could see the confidence in his walk and his demeanor. This made me think: this business must be good. We sat at my mother's kitchen table and he showed me a PowerPoint presentation of the business plan.

The day before I was calling it stupid and now, I was amazed by it. I couldn't wait to get started. I decided that this guy was sharp and could help me get off to a great start—plus he had a twin, so there were two of them! I also thought about the twin baby boys I had lost and now these twins were showing up in my life. I felt that this was the right team to be on; I called my mom's friend and explained I would not be joining the business.

I asked two questions: how do I start and when can I make $5000 a month? He told me I can start now and if I mastered the invitation and set appointments that I could make that money. They had only been in the business seven months and

88

their checks were $2000 a week. I had never known anyone my age that was making that type of money, let alone for putting 10 hours a week into the business. They were doing so well that they'd sold their car dealership. I was also realistic and told myself this could take five years—if you're going to do this, you are going to give it at least five years. I took out my credit card and joined the business for $300. My advice to people is to look at everything offered to you before you say no. After all, information changes situations.

I know nothing in life that's worth anything is free and I understood the company supplied me with tools, training and support which was very worth the startup cost. I also had a team of experienced leaders helping me and the ability to now have tax breaks. Within minutes, I had a website and I started to make calls. Within an hour, I had already triggered my first bonus check. My mother, my aunt and my coworker all wanted to use my service and that was my first $200 check, which has led to over 7-figures of income almost 6 years later.

I was told to make a contact list of potential customers and ask them to support my business. In the past, when someone tried to show me a network marketing business, I had a hard time asking people to spend money on a product I didn't believe in and that's why I never joined any of them. All of them were great companies with lots of success, they just weren't for me. The company I joined was an essential services company and offered services everyone needed and already used. Everyone also had the opportunity to be my customer free of charge, as well as saving money. I had no issues asking the people in my life to be my customer. I asked my friends, family, co-workers, and the people whose businesses I supported. I explained it would mean a lot to me and help me with my student loans.

Within a few weeks, I had 15 customers and to this day 13 of those 15 are still with me. I had a few people tell me no. One was my best friend at the time and a family member. They say inmates in prison don't want see other inmates escape. That also is true in life; many people who have given up on their dreams don't want to see others make it big. I also made a contact list of the people who I thought would want to make money. I started to call each one of them up excitedly and told them I had to show them what I was up to because it was going to be life-changing.

Some of the people I called knew me and had never heard me talk like this, so they agreed to meet with me. Others laughed and said: is it one of those pyramid things? I had never heard of a pyramid thing before, so I told them to just meet with me and decide for themselves. Within my first week, I showed the business to six people. The three people who were the ones I thought would do it said no.

One of them was a very close friend who I would help no matter what he needed. I was so close to him, I would have taken a punch for this guy. I was supposed to come show him the business and he called me and said, "I don't want to hear about this shit you're doing." I was hurt that he wouldn't at least let me show him but understood it wouldn't be for everyone. I asked him to just be my customer for free and save some money and he said no to that as well. At that moment, I realized maybe he really wasn't such a good friend. I was always helping him and never asked for anything until now. The second friend said no but he became my customer. After seeing my success for about four years and being tired of working his life away, he decided to join me.

The third guy I showed the business to got so excited. He said he was going to the bank to withdraw money to join me and never came back. Turns out his dad told him it was probably a scam. So my three home run hitters were all a "no" and the three who I really didn't think would do it signed up.

The exciting news was I was promoted to a leadership position in my first week and had tripled my investment. The bad news was that I was super confused why my first three didn't see what I saw. I started studying material on network marketing and looking at each one of the stories of the top earners in the company. I was surprised to find out it was an industry worth about $180 billion, that paid out about $70 billion a year to its distributors. The top earners didn't stand out to me; they all looked like ordinary people from all walks of life. After reading their stories, I realized they were all highly motivated people who wanted more out of life, so they took massive action and didn't believe in quitting.

I knew that I had to take massive action and just not quit no matter how many times I would hear the word no. I also told myself: life is going to throw its own challenges at me outside of this business, and I need to stay focused. I brushed off my three friends not joining and realized I didn't need a co-signer for my dreams.

What if I wanted to open a scuba diving business and people I knew didn't like scuba diving, would I shut down? Of course not! I would go out and make noise in the universe. Or what If I had a retail store and someone came in and looked around and walked back out, would I get offended? No. I would just think I don't have what that person wants but the next person may. I told myself this business is no different and that no will lead to yes. I started booking 5-10 meetings a week to show my new business with the help of my coaches, the twin brothers.

I thought about everyone I knew and reached out to them and I had a huge list. Out of every 10 people I approached about half wouldn't even message or call me back. Out of the other half, a few would say no and a few would say yes. I started noticing it was a numbers game, the law of large numbers, and there was no way with 700,000 people in my area that this couldn't work. So I had six new business partners fast. I focused more on team building and teaching everyone to each get a few customers. As a team, we got paid on all our customers combined. Soon I realized that all six of my teammates were not taking massive action and everyone had slowed down and quit. I got hit with my first dose of discouragement.

I had made a few thousand dollars at that point and was happy with the business but couldn't understand how I could get six people to add to the team and they couldn't. I thought there must be someone out there who was just as motivated as me. My seventh partner ended up building a team of 150 business partners; my eighth partner only got a few customers and my ninth partner built a team of over 50 business partners. This gave me more knowledge on how the business worked.

I realized the law of large numbers also worked for finding partners who would work the business like me. I was now promoted to a higher level of leadership and I was starting realize that leverage and residual income was much better than ordinary income from what I was used to. There were about five people who I had run into and spoke with about my new business and all agreed to sit with me so I could share the business with them.

When I followed up, all five had an excuse. I remember that day was the first time I ever thought about quitting. I went home and took a nap and when I woke up, I looked at all the top 25 money earners on the company's website again and told myself if they did it, I'm going to do it. I quit football in high school, I'm not quitting this. I had a few slow weeks and some small paychecks but I kept pushing, all while keeping a straight streak at college going and working at the spa and cutting lawns.

My personal life was still challenging but I knew that life is always going to be challenging. If I wait for the perfect moment in life when everything is right, it will never happen. I had to make this business part of my life, like brushing my teeth, not a choice but a duty. The following weeks lead me to some new people I met and some people I had forgotten about. I had a few new business partners join and within a few weeks had reached one of the highest leadership positions in the company. I had now reached the position of the twin brothers and had learned enough from them that I was now willing to run my business without their help.

I was now in the big leagues and if I could help many other people change their lives financially, at this leadership level, it would also change my life dramatically.

I remember thinking, I've helped people save money and helped other people make money; I've been promoted three times and earned three income increases, all in 90 days. I was also starting to get positive affirmations from many of the people in the company; people were starting to know my name. No job or traditional business that I was ever part of gave me this much. There was one major challenge though and it had me feeling that maybe I had gotten as far as I can. I had run out of contacts and everyone in my phone I had already contacted. Now that I could earn life-changing income at the higher level, I doubted myself.

My mind started to make reasons why the top money earners were probably successful. I figured they probably knew more people than I did or came across more people daily. My conscious mind was thinking and my subconscious was doing its job of always proving my conscious right. I decided to talk to my mother. She has been through many obstacles in her life that most people would have never gotten through. When she first wanted to open a day spa everyone around her told her it was a dumb idea and no one would come to get facials. She decided to sell the house we grew up in and take the equity to start her day spa. It was the first day spa in the town and she posted an ad in the local paper that she was giving first-time-free facials to women that came into her spa.

Women starting calling and coming into the spa and after a free facial they kept coming back. That was back in 1989 and in 2003, 14 years later, her spa was featured on the Oprah Winfrey show. As a kid, watching my mom's struggles in pursuit of her dreams taught me to never listen to naysayers and that success takes time. I recall the defining moment that exploded my business like it was yesterday. I came out of the bedroom and leaned over the second-floor balcony. My mother was sitting on the living room sofa. I told her that I didn't think I could do much more with the new business because I didn't know any more people. My mother encouraged me to not give up and explained that there were so many people out there looking for more out of life. I just had to make new relationships and get better at listening to people and building rapport. She told me to go outside my circle and put myself out there to the universe. That conversation gave me a new fire and a new plan of action. I was going to start building new friendships and become more outgoing with strangers. I have a friend who always says, "A stranger is a friend you haven't met yet." He's absolutely right.

Sitting here writing this, I'm thinking, imagine if I had quit? I don't even want to imagine my life if I didn't continue this opportunity.

In the next few months my success with strangers was amazing. I started getting new business partners from my local gym and off social media. My business was exploding and in my ninth month I was making over five figures a month. By month 11, I sold my lawn business and had the weekends to also focus on my network marketing business. The more I focused on it, the more it grew and the more money I made as a direct result of helping more people. By month 14, I had my first $20,000 month and over $100,000 saved in the bank. My goal was to stay working for my mother one more year and invest my savings into real estate. That same month the founder and CEO of the company called me to let me know I was an asset to the company. I was blown away, a multimillionaire calling me to tell me I was doing a great job? Because of the phone call, I walked into work a few minutes late; my mother gave me a hard time about showing up late. I got very upset and walked out, and that was my last day ever at a job.

Looking back now, I understand why I was so upset but I probably overreacted. My mother was so supportive of me building my network marketing business. As strict as she was, there were times where she would allow me to put a sign on the spa entrance that we were closed for an hour so I could run out and do a quick business presentation with a potential partner. She believed in me that much! The first two weeks without a job, I felt awkward, but after that I loved the time, freedom and owning my life. My mom gave me her blessing to move on from her salon after 12 years. She saw how much I enjoyed what I was doing. I can tell you, if you love what you do, it doesn't feel like work.

I now had the ability to work my business anytime I wanted to. The great thing about network marketing is that you can work as much or as little as you want. If you're consistent, it can be very lucrative. My girlfriend now is in the business with me which has even helped make our relationship more rewarding. She owns a busy hair salon and is a single mom and with only an hour or two a week she has added a significant amount of income to her life. The following month after quitting my job, I was promoted to the highest leadership level in the company. A few months later, I attended the company's major destination event and was ranked as one of the top 25 money earners in the company. If the honor itself wasn't enough, they also awarded me with a new Mercedes Benz.

My first destination event, the year before, really made it clear to me that I wanted to become a network marketing professional. I saw other associates of the business earning cars and ranking in the top 25 and my competitive nature erupted, full-force. I think if I didn't go to that first event, I would have still had success, but not the success I achieved by the following year. Joining my network marketing business has been one of the best things that ever happened to me. I have helped thousands of people get comfortable with being uncomfortable and change their mindsets, along with helping people save and make money.

I have earned more money in five years than I would have in 40 years working for myself and my mother. The relationships I've made are priceless. All my best friends I met because of this business, and I even met my girlfriend at a birthday party someone in the business was having. I've been awarded a Mercedes Benz for five years in a row and earned all-inclusive exotic trips each year. This year I earned a trip to Hawaii for a week, somewhere I have always wanted to go. Now I get to go and take my girlfriend too—all paid for by the company!

I am compensated for all my efforts and there is no capping out like in a traditional 9 to 5 work world. Working for myself with the lawn business, I could only put in so many hours a week. Working for my mom, no matter how much I helped the company grow, I was maxed out in pay.

Once you understand the power of residual income, you would walk through a brick wall to obtain it. There are famous actors and musicians who have passed away and their trusts still collect royalties. As amazing as it is, you will need thick skin to make it big. Most the people I coach make a few hundred to a few thousand dollars a month. Only a small percentage will create the kind of wealth I have. I have been active throughout my five years in the industry. I have continued to self-educate myself. I have continued to interact and build rapport with strangers and I have continued to grow my brand, which attracts people to want to do business with me. Anyone can do it; it's about wanting it bad enough.

So let's go over some of the cons to network marketing. It's not always glitter and gold, especially in the beginning. This information you won't be told until you're in the industry and find out for yourself. If you decide to follow my lead and start network marketing, this will be a mental preview for success. That is the misperception of people who are programmed to only understand making money by trading time for it. I would never put down someone's choice or how they make a living, but there are many out there who put down network marketing. I believe for many, it's a lack of information. It's easy to see why many have a negative impression of network marketing after being accosted by overzealous, amateur network marketers relentlessly trying to sell them something.

Your friends and family will most likely not want to join your business. In any business I have been a part of, my friends and family wanted free stuff or discounts. You can start there but be prepared to get good at listening and offering solutions to people. Some of the people you invite to see your business won't respond back to you. Be prepared for many cancelations and no shows.

Remember all experiences eventually will lead to people who will show up. Many of these people will be watching you and if you continue to have success without them, they will come back to you one day and ask you to show them your business. You will also experience those who will try to convince you that you're wasting your time. You will hear things like: "No one makes money with those things," "It sounds like one of those things," "It's a scam," "It's a pyramid scheme," "You're going to go to jail," "You're going to have to pay all the money you make back," and countless other ridiculous statements from people who have no clue about what you're doing.

Most of these people have never done network marketing or have not had success in it if they have. Every single person I have seen that has failed in this industry failed because of them, not the industry. There are also those who have given up on their dreams and are stuck at a job they dislike and because you're excited and telling them how amazing your life will be as you build this new business, it makes them attack you. It's their defense because if you have success it will make them look bad and they know they don't have what it takes to be successful. People can gain success one of two ways: they can follow you and earn it themselves or they can cut you down to their level and that makes them feel successful because you're not ahead of them.

I can tell you, this industry made me a stronger person, a better person, and I found out who my true friends were. I also found out a lot about the mentality of most people. There are many people who fear success, have fear of going outside their comfort zone, and can't handle rejection. When they decide to start their own business, these traits are a sure recipe for failure. If they are willing to overcome these traits and grow they can be very successful.

I wrote more than I initially intended to in this chapter but this chapter has led to the breakthroughs in my life. I know network marketing is not for everyone and my intentions are not to convince anyone that it is something they must do. For me, network marketing seems like it was created just for me. I love every aspect of it because I love people. Without people in life, there are no opportunities or positive affirmations. Positive affirmations are a key ingredient in helping people reprogram their subconscious mind which is stuck in its ways. In my five and a half years in this industry, I have probably shown my business to approximately 500 people. 170 joined me, 100 didn't do much at all and quit, 50 did it as a hobby, and 20 took it seriously and added over 4,000 partners and over 15,000 customers to my business, which helped change my financial circumstances.

I look at it as numbers game: the more numbers, the better the chance of winning. I had never done network marketing before and didn't have any education on it at all. I became one of the fastest money earners in my company because I didn't quit! I now laugh at the obstacles that arise and these are the same ones that used to upset me and make me discouraged. Whether it's network marketing or it's something else you're pursuing, never give up! It won't be easy, but I promise you, it will be worth it. You can't have a rainbow without riding out the storm first.

CHAPTER 12

WE MUST CONTINUE
TO EVOLVE

Your network is your net worth. I am still building my network marketing business and it will only continue to become more lucrative as the company grows. I'm a few months from earning another top 25 spot in the company and another year of Mercedes Benz car allowances. The business grows even without me these days, but I haven't slowed down. I still pursue new people to coach and am actively coaching over a dozen people, helping them follow my footsteps. What I have done is taken all the valuable information I have gathered along the way and followed the clues of successful people in the industry I met.

A few years ago, I started taking my extra bonuses that I was earning and investing them in real estate. I believe that you need multiple streams of income in this economy if you want to outlive your money. I often say multiple streams for multiple dreams. I don't believe you can be a top money earner in two network marketing businesses. If you chase two rabbits, you won't catch either. I am going to share with you how today I own 18 rentals and a fitness apparel business.

My original goal was to own 20 rentals but now I see myself going for 30. I have used about $500,000 of my network marketing income in the last five years and own a few million dollars in land. I love owning land because they are not making anymore. With about 70 million baby boomers retiring and not looking to buy houses and another 70 million millennials who are not interested in owning homes like their parents, it's a renter's market for many years to come.

We have only seen two real estate market collapses in the last 100 years and there were warning signs for those paying attention. Personally, I am not a fan of handing my money over to someone else to invest it. I like a tangible investment that I can see, touch, and manage myself. To think in 2011, I couldn't get a single bank to even loan me a dollar and today I am getting unsecured lines of credit left and right and using the banks money to create wealth.

Let me tell you step by step how I did it. I am not a professional real estate guru and am not telling you what to do or giving you advice, I am merely telling you how I have had success in real estate. I come across so many people who want to start getting into real estate and I use my network marketing business to help them get the capital to start. Therefore, I am going to give an overview of what I did.

In 2012, I tried getting a loan for an investment property and I was not approved. My 2010 and 2011 tax returns were horrible. I made 20k with my network marketing business in 2011 but I didn't make enough income for what the banks wanted. In 2012, I made six figures for the first time in my life but the year was not over and I didn't have tax returns yet. I decided to buy a property for $78,000 cash, which had been sold to the previous owner for $300,000 a few years back before the real estate bubble popped. I still had my original house and that was rented by the same tenant, since I had been forced to move in with my mother in 2008 and rent my house or lose it.

This was the only real estate experience I had and I made about $200 profit each month on my own house. My goal was to make $200-$300 per door that I would own. I also used a formula of dividing my net yearly profit on a rental by how much money came out of my pocket to obtain it. This would tell me how much my money was making annually compared to the less than 1 percent the savings account was making me.

So let's say I bought a house for $50,000 and with 20 percent down, closing and a few repairs, I spent $16,000. The rent is $1,000 a month and $300 of that is net profit each month after all expanses. I am in my goal range of $200-300, and now to find out my annual percentage profit I use this formula: 12 months multiplied by $300 net profit which gives me $3,600. Then I divide that by my $16,000 out of pocket expenses. This gives me a 22.5 percent return on my money. Formulas are just guides to give you an idea if you're on the right track.

Assuming I don't have crazy big repairs, I have my investment back in about five years and the only money left at risk is the banks money. Can you save $16,000 and in five years have your $16,000, plus something worth $50,000? Of course not. And land will never be worth zero, like a stock can be.

Once I got my 2012 tax returns, I made a game plan to acquire a few properties that year. Thanks to my financial earnings in my network marketing business, I no longer paid my bills late and my credit score was back in the 700s. I moved into my condo so that I could get a home equity line of credit and started looking for real estate to purchase. My goals were to buy three properties and use the line of credit for the 20 percent deposit and the bank for the other 80 percent.

On December 31, 2013, I closed on three single homes and a duplex in Allentown, Pennsylvania. I went from one tenant to six overnight and I have no skills as a handyman. What I do have is people skills and management team building skills. I don't look at my tenants as just tenants; they are part of my team to manage a business. In the beginning, I got stressed when I would get a call that something was wrong at one of my rentals. Then one day I had a mind shift, I told myself this is no different than when I worked for my mom and an employee called and told me there was an issue.

In 2014, I used the rest of the line of equity on my condo and bought an investment property in Bethlehem, Pennsylvania. I started a new Limited Liability Company (LLC) for the new county. Having my properties in an LLC gives me liability protection from being personally liable. The banks also give better interest rates for lines of unsecured credit to a business than when it's in a person's name.

Many banks won't allow you to cash out on equity after the fourth house bought in your name and after 10 houses they will cut you off on loans. At this point, I started hearing about flipping houses. Some of my friends were already doing it. There was profit in it but I wanted to have a four-wealth system not just one. Flipping houses seemed like a job to me. You buy the house, do work on it, and then sell it, hoping the market is in your favor, then you do it all over again. Nothing wrong with that and for some who can't get loans this is a great way to start. I like having cash flow, my mortgage being paid down, equity being built and tax advantages. I continued to buy and hold for long term wealth.

In the following years, I bought many of my properties with unsecured lines of credit or credit cards that offer a three percent one-time fee and no interest for 12 months. If I want to get the house off the market, I will use my line to buy it as cash, and have a fast close which gets me a better deal on the house. My bank allows me the following month to put a mortgage on it for 70 percent loan to value. This gives me a good amount of my money back. I use the cash flow to payback the borrowed lines and or the credit card and I keep repeating this process. The more real estate I own the more velocity I create and the faster I can keep following this system.

Along the way, there have been challenges that I expected and many that I didn't. I have dealt with a bed bug infestation, emergencies, drug raids, late rent, an eviction and other issues. Most of these issues are my own fault as my system was not a great system. I realized I was allowing some of these issues to happen, and as I changed my system my results got better. It will never be perfect. You're dealing with people and everyone is very different. If you like people and you like managing people, then you can create lots of wealth in real estate. As I have grown my real estate investing, I also have a team of professionals who all play an important role in its success; the banks, the accountant, the lawyer, the insurance company, the real estate agent, the contractors, the title company and my supportive girlfriend. Even if I get one call a day, five days a week, it's worth the freedom of being home and not working somewhere I don't love.

Sometimes, I have no issues for a few weeks at a time and other times I am asking myself why I even started this. That is completely normal in life: as our stress levels rise and emotions come into play, logic goes down. At the end of the day, no risk, no reward and scared money doesn't make money. I would rather lose it all and know I tried than one day looking back and regretting I never took a chance in life. If you decide to get into real estate I urge you to read some of the top books out there about investing in real estate.

Just like network marketing, people will try to talk you out of it. One of my bankers urged me to not get into real estate and if I did, then only buy one property. Another friend told me all the horror stories he knew and that I was going to regret it. A few years later these two guys are still in the same exact spot and I have built a small fortune that I plan to allow the next generation to have my last name to take advantage of. The people who always told me to not pursue my dreams work for their first name. I work for my last name.

In April 2016, I had the privilege of meeting Robert Herjavec in Dallas, Texas, at a destination event for my network marketing company. After listening to his story and talking with him, I realized I was not as busy as I thought. I was basing my action on the people who spent the most time in my home town. He opened my eyes to the fact that the most successful people are moving at warp speed. It's the fast that eat the slow in this economy, not the big that eat the small. I needed to move faster and take advantage of the gift of time. I am young and healthy, and if I don't hustle like crazy now, I never will. Massive action creates massive long term success. On the plane ride home, one of best friends in my network marketing business and I discussed that we needed to do more. We're both fitness enthusiasts and appreciate fitness apparel. We decided we would start a motivational and positive fitness apparel company. We started writing down names and ideas right away. As soon as we got home, we formed the company and started to get to work. Every step of the way we were faced with challenges. Some of them were because the people we hired didn't have the same work ethic as we did and it was all new to us.

We were learning as we grew the business. I believe when it comes to acting on a new venture, when you jump, you earn your wings on the way down. Too many people try to perfect everything before they start and end up failing before they start. The universe will never give you success until it sees you took a chance and put your own skin in the game first. We launched the clothing line only two months later and it's been a huge success with the local area we live in. We have been invited to all the major gyms in the area and have been getting most of our sales online through social media. The clothing industry has its challenges as there is a lot of inventory that may not sell.

There are also so many people starting clothing lines these days. I never let anything or anyone stop me from doing what I believe in and you never should either. It's been a fun business and we have met so many people we would have never met. It's growing my network and creating relationships for the future. The feeling when you see someone wearing something that was just a thought in your mind is priceless.

It's been six years now that I have been able to use my mind shift and new belief system to transform my life. There are many people much more successful than me and always will be. This is not about how successful you are, it's about knowing that you're not stuck where you are. With the right thinking, you can transform your life, no matter what your past was like. I had two choices: to allow my past to lead me down that dark road, or to take the punches life threw at me and stand up and move forward.

My future is up to me as yours is up to you. I continue to make choices that lead me closer to my goals. If I do that, I know the next six years will lead me to an even better place. Things will go wrong, I will make mistakes, and people close to me may even get sick or die. There will be times I feel beat up but I can't allow myself to live in those moments too long, as I used to years ago. There are things going on in my life, at the time of writing this book, that would have the average person focusing so much on them that they would not be focusing on their goals. Once you can learn to stay on course no matter what happens in your life, you will always be moving forward.

Too many people are moving forward in a circle and ending up in the same place. As we move up the levels of success, every new level will have another devil. What that means is that as you have more people around you and you are financially successful, there will be more temptations of new things that can bring you back to rock bottom. I am always on the lookout for these dangerous distractions that could lead to my demise. There are countless people who had it all and lost it all.

CHAPTER 13

TIME FOR A
PARADIGM SHIFT

The next two chapters are going to help you learn some new ideas to jump to the next level. I truly believe you can never stop learning because life never stops teaching. I have a lot more to learn in my lifetime. I want you to learn how to be someone who exudes passion, confidence and a positive contagious energy. If you are always the smartest person in the room, it's time for a new room. I'm asked often, what is the one single thing that I attribute to my success? There is no 'single' thing that gave me success.

The first thing, however, was thinking big positive thoughts of what I wanted in life and not what I was lacking. Positive thoughts lead to a positive life and negative thoughts lead to a negative life. It really is that simple. I started to become solution-oriented rather than problem-focused. I made a choice to change my life and committed to it. The choice to change was relatively quick but the change itself took longer to manifest, only after I took consistent action. I started to change my thinking and become more grateful for what I had beginning every morning as I awoke. The key from here was to pick the right daily mundane activities that would eventually compound into success.

I mentally rehearsed all the possible downfalls and prepared myself for them. Then each day I would do a few things that would allow me to be a tiny bit closer to my goal of success. Looking back now, it may seem like it was an overnight success but it was simply the daily little positive things and time management. I also started having self-awareness of who I was and became clearer on what I wanted out of life. I realized I couldn't hit a target that I couldn't see.

I wrote the next part of this book to help you develop more positive thinking and habits of positive actions. This is the first step to change. Our country is based on freedom. That freedom was once just a thought and a group of individuals acted on that thought and today we have the freedom to be anything we want. Everything in life starts as a formless substance we call a thought! Writing this book started as a thought. The laptop I'm typing on was once someone's thought. The company who will publish my book was once a thought. All these thoughts needed action and that action causes a ripple effect in many more lives for many years.

My success all started simply by reading some simple quotes every day and started to believe in these positive words I read daily. Simple little positive words made me think that perhaps there is something to being positive. The natural state of a garden is weeds; the natural state of the brain is negativity. You read firsthand all my past issues and challenges. You have your own past and issues you have experienced. Some of you may be still going through them. It's time to let all that go and give yourself 21 days—you owe it to yourself. I have designed a simple and duplicable 21-day program to assist you with your own mind shift. This positive daily quote program is a simple and effective way to get you thinking positively and invigorate your creativeness to start working again. It doesn't matter what your past is or where you are today at this very moment. We all have the chance to change our circumstances. Take a deep breath right now! What do you feel? Yes, you feel air but more importantly you feel alive. You are alive! This means you have not completed what you are supposed to complete. This means you have time to learn more, do more, and be more. This also means your current reality is only temporary and by producing new grateful and positive thoughts everything about your life can and will change for the better.

This is a great book for those who want a stronger positive outlook on life but don't know where to start or for those who just want to enjoy a book written from the heart. If you want to create more positive thoughts in your daily life, you can with this simple 21-day guide I'm going to share with you in the following chapter. These daily quotes and simple exercises can help anyone to improve their output. Become a more positive you and you will attract the abundance the world has to offer. You can't have a positive life with negative thinking. People who think negative will contaminate you. If that is true, then being around those who think positively and look at life with gratitude will also contaminate you for the better.

What we read, who we spend time with, what we listen to, what we watch on TV is all a direct result of how we speak, dress, feel and think about ourselves. I choose to not allow all the negativity to fill my mind to what life can offer. Instead, I choose to read things and spend time with people who stretch me and help improve my character.

I believe we are an average of those whom we associate with

the most. I would never tell anyone that they must not associate with anyone who's a family or friend who may be negative. But you can limit that time spent with them (also known as limited association) or simply add positive things to your life to offset the negative things. My belief is that we can only have positive achievements in life with positive thinking. Negative thoughts never create positive results. To change our circumstances, we must change our thinking. If you keep thinking the same, you will always get the same results. We can create a new positive habit in only 21 days. I have created this exercise and the quotes to help you reprogram your mind. These simple daily actions can get your mind thinking positively and help you achieve a more successful life. A happier you will make for a happier life as well as for the people around you. You may not see results the first day, or the first week, but if you give it the full 21 days, this seemingly insignificant daily activity will compound into something you can really gauge.

My long-term goal for you is to live a vibrant, happy, and fulfilling life and I am confident this can be your catalyst. After the 21 days of this program, your brain should crave positive thoughts and you will on your own look for uplifting quotes, videos, poems and books to consume on a daily basis as congruent with your more positive self. It won't take the same will power as it did on day one. Think about taking the garbage out or brushing your teeth—that took will power in the beginning. Now it's like second nature and doesn't demand any willpower since it's now on autopilot. I wake up every day with the desire to learn something new, offering me redeemable value and wanting to learn more tomorrow than I did today.

It's still very beneficial if I only have two minutes on some days to invest into my personal development. Our mind is the most powerful tool we have. People have beat odds and accomplished the impossible all because of their mind believing they could. It doesn't matter who you are, where you came from, or what you now know. It's all about being positive, consistent, disciplined and having faith. For the next 21 days allow yourself to believe in yourself. Give yourself the chance you deserve to grow as a person. Our success is up to us, and only us. But it makes it easier having the tools or blueprint to follow to your destination without having to experience all the bumps on the road. We must show up to go up and this is your chance to show up.

Before you start the 21-day program, let me leave you with a few more things. Your conscious mind is the thinker and the subconscious mind is the prover. This means the conscious part of your brain makes thoughts. The job of the subconscious is to prove those thoughts right. So if you tell yourself "I can't get ahead in life," your subconscious will make reasons for you so that it proves your conscious mind correct; I'm too young, I'm too old, I'm not smart, I come from a broken home, my parents never had success, and so on.

By understanding this relationship and by stepping outside yourself in a sense and watching your thoughts, you can really derail negative things from happening to you and start to use your subconscious to prove your positive thoughts right. If you drive to work and think I hate my job, trust me your subconscious will come up with many reasons to prove you right and prove why you hate your job. It becomes a self-fulfilling prophecy. Ultimately you are creating your own worst reality. The hardest challenge in a human's life is the conquering of one own self. When you catch yourself thinking negatively and you stop it before the subconscious can prove you right.

That is the crucial step to conquering yourself!

As Leonardo da Vinci said, "One can have no smaller or greater mastery than mastery of oneself."

———————

CHAPTER 14

GK'S 21 DAY PROGRAM

Here are the simple steps to follow for the next 21 days. I recommend doing a program like this at least twice a year, every
six months. I do something daily and always use my daily 20-
40 minutes walking on the treadmill or cardiovascular session
on the recumbent bike to read. This has allowed me to be able
to read one to two books a month. Reading for one day won't
change your life but when you do it every day, you will have
read 10-20 good self-help books at the end of the year. Reading
that many books consistently and habitually every day will pro-
foundly change your life, trust me!

This 21-day system of positive thoughts, the daily reading
and action-oriented lifestyle have trained my mind to know
how to take advantage of the great things life has to offer. I now
can only function if I wake up every day and do something positive. I understand everyone's life is different. But keep in mind,
most of the things we worry about are never going to happen,
already happened, or the worries are our insecurity about what
others think of us. None of those things we can control. So it's
about changing our perspective and our focus on the things
that can happen, which is a very small percentage.

If you worry a lot or get stressed often it's because you are smart and creative, really. Smart and creative people think a lot. Once you make logical sense of the things in your life it's as easy as redirecting your creativity and your focus on what we can control. One thing that helps me a great deal is asking myself if this problem or issue will still be important in a week, month or year? If the answer is "No," then I visually see myself a week, month or year from now and that problem is nowhere in sight. This technique has allowed me to free up my mind from unwanted worry and stress.

Get up every day and write down things you are grateful for or even start out your day with this book—it will help you redirect your stress and worries that may be consuming your life. I don't want to be the bearer of bad news but even when you have all the money, all the success, and all the love in the world there will still be problems. In fact, the only thing that interrupts problems in life is the occasional crisis. Most people reading this book are in a crisis, about to be in one or just got out of one. The good news is that becoming a positive thinking individual who can control their thoughts and learn to be solution-oriented can handle these challenges that life will give you and pass with straight A's! Ok, I don't know about you but I'm ready to start this new exciting journey of immediate action and change. So let's get started, shall we!

Step 1

Read one quote a day and my personal story that's connected with the quote. Read the quote three times to yourself, so you really break it down in your brain. Read it aloud if that helps you retain better.

Step 2

Write the quote down on the space provided. I believe a good old-fashion pen or pencil is still the most effective way to learn. Write a short explanation on how your life is affected already by the quote and what you could do to change things to obtain a positive result in life in the space provided.

Once you are finished, allow yourself to see your life as if this change has already taken place. Daydream for a minute as if you are watching yourself having that positive result. This is very powerful activity for change. This will allow you to start thinking differently and getting your brain to work in a different way. This will cause the brain to develop new connections for growth. New growth can lead to more possibilities of creativity and new energy. Energy attracts energy. As you become more positive you will notice more positive things and people start to come into your life. You will be attracting these things to you by the positive person you are becoming.

By writing what you could do to change things, you are becoming solution-oriented and brain storming. More importantly, my belief is you are putting it out into the universe. If you want to have something happen in life you must let that thought loose. You must also do everything twice, not literally, but once in your mind and once for real. You must see what you either want or want changed as the final result has already taken place. Always remember, energy flows where attention goes.

Your life will move in the direction of your dominant thoughts. For example, after reading quote 1 of the book, I would write something like this:

"The people at my gym I talk to are really negative about life and about my goals that I've shared with them. I think I need to start hanging out with new people who share my dreams and vision." Now after writing this, I mentally picture myself in a room laughing and discussing my goals with others who think what I have to say is great. The thought of this makes me smile and gives me hope to find like-minded people. This now makes me want to find those people. I decide to look online for local groups who have meetings who share my same visions. This now leads to new action and immediate change. By then going to a meeting of like-minded people, I've just opened a new opportunity for my life and endless possibilities. This step allows you to put your thoughts on paper, which is the first step to solving problems and forces you to see right in front of your eyes what is really going on in your life. It clarifies the current energy going on in your life and gives you a sense of clarity.

Step 3

The best gift of all is giving back to others. Zig Ziglar famously shares, "If you help enough other people get what they want, you can have everything you want." This is where we give back to others. It's now time to share the quote with at least three people. This will put a positive energy out in the atmosphere and give someone new input they normally would not have gotten if it were not for you. If they share it with others, which you should encourage them to do with at least three people, a ripple effect will be produced. Even if they don't share it, you are going to create a happy, positive new life by doing a good deed.

People will notice this new sense of energy about you in the a few weeks and when they ask you why you are so happy, you can share with them how that little quote you sent them was not as little as it looked. At this point, other people who may not have shared it may now have their lives improved by you as you share the knowledge of this book.

Remember it was a few simple quotes that started the positive change in my life and the fuel for me writing this book. As it makes a positive change for you it can and will do the same for others. One small action like this can lead to something so big you may not even currently comprehend. Imagine someone changes their thinking and it leads them to start taking action. They get around new positive people, opportunities start to come their way, they start believing in themselves and they decide to become comfortable with being uncomfortable. Next thing you know because of their new thinking they finally have started the new company they always wanted to but were too overwhelmed with negativity and worry to even have a chance. They add something to our economy that's valuable to society and they create jobs for thousands of people. And it all started with a positive quote. A simple social media re-post can be the message that someone needs to see that's the catalyst to change their life. You can simply email it, text it or post it on a social media website. A simple minute out of your day could help so many people in need of a message that could be exactly what they needed to change their situation that day.

Step 4

The most important step is the action step: putting in motion what you need to do. This act will help you achieve a positive result. In step 2, you are stating and visualizing what you think you need to do for the quote to help you. Now in step 4, you are writing down your action and performing the action. It doesn't have to be that same day but make an entry in your calendar for when you act on that quote. Thoughts without action cannot form into reality. There is no power in intentions. I intended to read a book is not reading the book. If there are three frogs sitting on the lake's edge and one decides to jump off onto an appealing lily pad, how many frogs are left? There are still three frogs there! Deciding to do something and doing it are not the same.

Many people decide to go to the gym, decide to eat healthy, decide to read a book, decide to be nicer to their significant other but until they actually take the necessary action and do it, they are no farther ahead than the two other frogs who never decided anything. Even if the frog imagines how nice it would be to sit on that lily and how nice the view is from there would be, if it doesn't act, it's just another frog that didn't allow itself a fair chance to make for a better life. Because as easy as it is to go to the gym, eat healthy, compliment your significant other, or read a book, and in the case of the frog take the leap to the lily pad, it's just as easy not to do those things.

This system I've devised is so easy to do, but it's also so easy not to do. This is where you need to dig deep inside your greatness and master the right daily activities. Realize that although one day of following this program isn't going to change your life or give you immediate results, that doesn't mean you should not take it seriously. Everything in life from getting in shape, becoming healthier, gaining success, or developing a great relationship are all a result of small daily actions compounded over time. Day 1 of the gym, eating healthy, meeting someone new you know you really like is very different than day 21 of those same situations.

Here is an example, after reading quote 1, of how I would take action:

"There is a positive person on my social media page that is always running events. I will make the effort to go to one of his events rather than hangout with my negative usual circle of people every weekend." If this is your answer, you must go to the event not only decide to go. I recommend taking action as soon as possible. Mark it on your calendar because I believe if it's not in your daily calendar, it's not in our life and won't get accomplished. Whatever you choose is what you must follow through on with action!

These four steps can really help you start thinking positively and get you making the necessary actions to help change your life. For us to change, a program with goals must be implemented. We can use any 21 quotes and have success but here are the 21 quotes I have personally created that really helped me in my life. Just follow the simple steps each day for 21 days to a new happier you. If you miss a day, just keep going in order until you finish. I would rather see someone do 1 quote a week on their day off for 21 weeks than nothing at all. Just give it your best because you deserve the best. These positive changes in our lives can only last if we do them regularly. It's like bathing—it must be done daily. If you catch yourself falling back into a negative pattern in a few months or a few years, just repeat this program. If you are doing better than ever after this book, you can always repeat the steps as a refresher. What you will find is that this book will be the first step to many more great steps in your life that are waiting for you!

1

"Another person's negative belief in you should never become your reality. Surround yourself with positive people that help you grow into a better you."

In my life, I have had people not believe in what I believed in. Some laughed, ridiculed, and told me I was wasting my time going for such big dreams. I always believed in my heart that their thinking was not going to change my thinking. It wasn't until I got around successful, positive people with similar goals that my dreams and thoughts manifested into everything I knew they would one day. We are a product of the company we keep and sometimes we must change the people around us to create the life we want.

2

*"Procrastination will kill your dreams and
all chances of success. Life will pass you by, it won't wait
for you as you did for it."*

I think the biggest success killer is waiting for everything in your life to perfect. I did this for many years and new issues just kept replacing the old ones. Time is something we can never get back and in my opinion the most important commodity we have. We need to have the courage to push through the pain and start our goals even when life is not where we want it to be.

3

"Why do you wake up each morning?
Why should anyone care? Find that "why" and many will care."

Our "why" in life can be the biggest asset to us. Money is a result and when the going gets tough money is not always enough to keep us battling through the tough times. A bigger reason like a better life, giving our kids a better life, and just rising above our current circumstances to show the world we can shine like a star. We need to share our why with the world and we will see many doors open for us.

4

*"You will need to go through a maze of failures
to get to the side of success."*

Success is like a rollercoaster, with ups and downs. It is very seldom a linear progression. At times, we will fail at ventures but we will take knowledge from each disappointment. One day we will find our niche and all those prior failures will be the reason why we finally succeeded and on much grander scale than ever before.

....

....

....

....

....

....

....

....

....

5

"When no one believes in you, it only means you're on the right track. Remember you don't need a co-signer for your dreams."

In life, we will sometimes experience a situation where the 'prisoners don't want to see the other inmates escape the prison.' This means that some people want you to do good but not better than them. I've learned that when I do something that most people disagree with, I am onto something big. Be daring enough to step outside the norm and your comfort zone. If some humans didn't do 'this' we would still be living in caves.

6

*"You have been given the gift of two hands for a reason.
One to help yourself and one to lift others up."*

I believe that if you help others it always comes back to you. This was reinforced by my mother at an early age. Helping others is rewarding and makes the world a better place. After the houses, the cars, the vacations, the awards, and the money, if you're not helping others achieve a better life than what do you really have? The more success we achieve the more privileged we become to help even more people.

7

*"Knowledge is strength and learning changes situations.
To grow we must be willing to learn more tomorrow
than we know today."*

My success increased as I read books and acquired more knowledge. I am a true believer that our financial success can never exceed our personal development. We must grow into the income or the person we want to be. A person who stops learning has stopped growing. Don't say if it's not broke don't fix it. Say if it's not broke how we can make it better.

8

"We must experience discouragement and setbacks to get to the end of the road of success."

I have started every venture before there was ever a taste of success. There were many discouraging moments and times I felt I was failing. I realized after several ventures that I always experienced these feelings but it always led to success. We must embrace the discouragement and feelings of failure because this is what comes before success. Each challenge will strengthen us and mold us into a better version of ourselves.

9

"To achieve success, we must see what we are not,
before we are."

I have always had a vision of what I was going to accomplish before I even started. Acting as if you have already achieved your goal will help you grow into your success. Start acting as if you already have made it to the top. Don't wait until you reach the top to show the world your greatness—start showing it on the road to success.

10

"I had to do it twice to become successful.
Once in my mind and once for real."

In 2011, I wrote out the story of how I wanted my life to unfold. The house I lived in, the car I drove, the lifestyle I lived. I wrote it as if it already had happened and I had a vision board with all those things I wanted to achieve it. Only 18 months later, I achieved every single thing on that list and they are no longer just dreams. The life I wrote about I am now living because I saw it first before it even happened. Our brain is the most powerful tool we have. Whether we tell ourselves that 'we can do' or 'cannot do,' we are right.

11

"Money doesn't make you wealthy, knowledge does."

Many times in my life, I chased wealth only to end up with nothing. It was not until I realized that to earn wealth I needed knowledge and lots of it. I had to be patient and outlast time and the money would come pouring in. Understanding how money works is something I was never taught in school. Now with the knowledge I have and continue to learn I have been able to make money work for me rather than me work for money. The more we learn and master, the more wealth we can acquire. I believe the wealth of a man is not the amount in his bank account but the amount of people he helped along the way to creating that wealth.

12

"In my eyes, a television is an electronic income reducer."

I would pick a book or audio book over a television any day. Being consumed with too much TV can make our minds shut off from growth. Long-term personal development is much more rewarding than instant gratification. Just like our bodies need exercise and nourishing foods, our brain needs mental exercise and good brain food. To be successful, we need to do more things that give us redeemable value, like creating this book for you to read instead of watching television. My choice today will create redeemable value for many. Five to six times a week, I do a fast walk on the treadmill and read about 10-20 pages of a good book. I never enjoyed reading but I have acquired an appetite for it. It has helped my life so much; that I now look forward to reading. You will always find a book in the side crack of my car seat.

13

"True peace in life can only come from finding a way to only work to live and not live to work."

Most of my life, I lived to work. I spent countless hours of my life at a job or running my own business. I traded time for money and my business owned me. It wasn't until I found out about network marketing and real estate investments that for the first time in my life worked to live. I believe to be a free human being we need to find ways to acquire passive residual income. This will allow you to need active income less and eventually not at all. Only then will we fully have financial and time freedom in life. Find someone who has already done this and follow their steps. Success leaves clues and getting around others who are more successful than you are is the best way to catch the success bug.

14

"We can choose to focus on despair, or we can focus on making ourselves stronger. The quantity of effort is the equal."

I realized as I started to grow into the person I am today that if I dwelt on the bad things in my life it took the same effort as it would to focus on the positive things instead. I started to shift my concentration on growing myself rather than continuing to be a prisoner by the bad in my life. We need to be careful about what thoughts we allow our mind to dwell upon and store for us to harvest. Negative thoughts will produce a negative life and positive thoughts will produce a positive life. Change your focus and you can change yourself.

15

"When just the dream is no longer adequate,
you will make it a reality."

Many of us have dreams about how we want our life to unfold. The house, car, vacation, and lifestyle we want to live. But for many of us it will only ever be just that, a dream. We never go from the dream to how to obtain that lifestyle. For me, one day, the dream was not enough, it was time to make a precise set of goals and turn my dream into reality. Only those who are not satisfied with just the dream will ever make their dreams come true. Our thoughts must become actions and only then will our life manifest into what we want. If you read this book but take no action, nothing will change. Many of us will not pursue our dream in the fear of failing and ruining that perfect image of it. Only those courageous enough will take the chance. You must keep your eyes on the prize no matter what happens to you along the journey.

16

"We have to practice running before the big race."

In life, we will not always succeed on the first attempt. Most of the best accomplishments that have changed the world took several failed attempts. We cannot learn anything without mistakes. We must keep trying and one day our time will come. The question is whether we'll be ready for it when it does happen. Every failed attempt is one attempt closer to victory.

17

"Action is the first step to change."

We can talk about change until we are blue in the face. We can set goals and have vision boards every year. Without action, none of the things we want in life will ever happen. Taking action can change your life overnight; it is the first step in achieving success. Without action, success is just a thought and it will never assume form. I thought about writing a book for years but never acted. Without me finally taking action, I would not have been able to help inspire people and you wouldn't be reading this book. Action is powerful beyond measure.

18

"A thought is a formless substance which all life stems from."

Everything created in our lives, or in the world for that matter, started with a thought. Someone had a tiny idea and they took it as far they could. Now having learned how powerful thoughts are, I am more aware of what I create in my life out of just an idea. I always do things in my life twice, once in my mind and once for real. I take that formless substance and playback in my head until I see the desired result. I make myself see the journey before I even start. I also mentally rehearse the challenges so when they arise, I am ready. If you think it, you can create it. That also goes for negative thinking. Many of us tell our thoughts and sabotage our lives. Next time you have an idea, realize you have the power to make it a reality.

19

"You must change your input to change your output."

Many of us want to change our lives and our circumstances but we continue to get up every day and do the same thing we have always done. The years pass and we never get ahead, we feel stuck. The best way to change our life is to change what we are doing. The frequency must be changed to cause new circumstances. In life, people give up positive affirmations and opportunities. When I was stuck, I decided my current path at work was not getting me to where I wanted to be. I had one of those moments where I was sick and tired of being sick and tired.

Some of the things I did were: join a new gym, take some college classes, volunteer at a church, start an online business, and read a book. All these things allowed me to do new activities, meet new people, and my life started to change. If you find yourself in a rut, do something new that will cause you to create a new path in life. If it scares you, then you are on the right path for growth.

20

"The only person that can stop you from having success or a good life is the person looking back at you in the mirror."

It's easy to blame our circumstances, past, or lack of success or a good life on others. Regardless of what has happened to you, it's your own responsibility to create the life you want. The excuses and the blame game must go away. Once you can accept responsibility a whole new world will open for you. It would have been easy for me to blame English being my second language as why I can't do great in English, but instead, I got tutors and in college got straight A's in all my English classes. I could have easily grown up to blame living in a disruptive and abusive home on why I couldn't break that pattern of abuse, but instead, I took responsibility for my own actions.

Start today and no longer point the finger at anything or anyone else. Remember, when you point the finger at someone, three fingers point back at you.

21

"Energy will travel to where your focus goes; your life will lean towards the direction of that focus."

We manifest what we focus the most on. If you're giving your focus to positive things, you will produce positive results. If you focus on the negative things in life, you will develop more negative things in your life. Time is the great equalizer. Things manifest by your will in life by focus or lack of it. If you focus your energy on things that can make you successful and go through that pain now, that energy and focus will create a great future. If you focus your energy on instant gratification, you will enjoy the present but suffer at the end of your life. Time will make you pay with pain plus interest. Be aware what you're putting your energy into and what people you're giving your time to. Have laser beam focus on the things that are working for you in life; or the things that you need to be doing.

If you got this far it means you read my book and I appreciate that. Writing a book for me was very hard but nothing in life that's easy is ever rewarding. My goal was that you gained a redeemable value by you purchasing this book. I started this book in 2013; I was about three chapters into it up until 2016. My GK 21-day program was the easiest part of the book for me to write. The positive fun stuff is always easier. Every time I started to write, the memories brought me back to a place I didn't want to be. I also heard that little voice in the back of my head telling me that I am not a writer and no one is going to want to read my book. This is that little voice in our head we all have. It likes to rear its ugly head in life when we are trying to do great things. That little voice has killed millions of dreams and that little voice is always wrong!

I would tell myself that I will cut out an hour a week out of my life and write until the book was complete. I did it only once each year in 2014 and 2015. From the first year I started writing, finishing my book was one of my New Year goals. A goal I failed to achieve each year. Or as I like to say, I was failing forward. Then in late 2016, Brian, my friend of 16 years, came into town and we went for lunch. As we were eating he looked at me and said, "You need to write that book." Something in his voice and the look in his eyes woke me up. I started to write with a sense of urgency that I never had before.

Each day I took the time to write. I was now more committed in finishing this book than ever before. I believed that this could be an opportunity to help others. I once read all successful people have one thing in common: they take immediate action when they see a great opportunity. As the New Year came and 2017 was here, I told myself this is the year. The year I finally do it!

I believe at the time of us setting goals, we truly believe that we can achieve them. Unfortunately, life is not always in cooperation with our goals. If your goals are not met, it's okay. You keep trying and one of these times, the timing and the right inspiration will be in your favor and you will succeed. A change in your life or a person may inspire you in a way that you never expected. But that will never happen if you quit. The time is going to pass either way. Have the time pass with you achieving what you desire. One thing I have learned about commitment is that without it nothing is completed in life. What I mean is, doing what you said you were going to do, long after the feeling that you said it in is gone. Understand that the initial feeling will always fade. You must focus on the result you wish to have fulfilled.

I actually wrote the 21 quotes first. I am glad that it took me this long to write the book because I could write much more of my positive life experiences over the last few years. I exposed a lot of the things in my life that I always kept locked up inside because they were uncomfortable. I decided to share my life and be vulnerable because I believe this is in service to others, as others have helped me in ways both big and small.

I can tell you that at this very moment, I do not have an editor, publisher or even a title for this book. If I focus too much on the unknowns it will never happen, like most things in life.

I have faith that I will find everything I need along the way because my passion for creating this book and helping others is that strong. I once heard that if a person embarks on a journey, that even if they don't have the right knowledge or people to help them, if they believe enough, they will always find those things. If you are reading this, it means that is true and it will be true for you too! Let's make the rest of your life, the best of your life.

To your success, health, and happiness!